D0119269

Creative CONTAINERS

Creative
CONTAINERS

Inventive Ideas for Pots, Windowboxes
and Hanging Baskets

Paul Williams

Trafalgar Square Publishing

First published in the United States of America in 1997 by Trafalgar Square Publishing
North Pomfret, Vermont 05053

Printed in Hong Kong and bound in China

First published in Great Britain in 1997 by Conran Octopus Limited
37 Shelton Street, London WC2H 9HN

Text copyright © 1997 Paul Williams
Design and layout copyright © 1997 Conran Octopus Limited

The right of Paul Williams to be identified as Author of this Work has been asserted by him in accordance
with the Copyright, Designs and Patents Act 1988.

All rights reserved. No part of this book may be reproduced, stored in a retrieval system, or transmitted in any
form or by any means, electronic, electrostatic, magnetic tape, mechanical, photocopying, recording or otherwise,
without the prior permission in writing of the Publisher.

COMMISSIONING EDITOR Stuart Cooper
PROJECT EDITOR Helen Ridge
ASSISTANT EDITOR Tessa Clayton
COPY EDITORS Sarah Sears, Anne de Verteuil
ART EDITOR Sue Storey
SPECIAL PROJECTS PHOTOGRAPHED BY Georgia Glynn-Smith
PICTURE RESEARCH Julia Pashley
PRODUCTION Sue Bayliss

ISBN 1-57076-075-6

Library of Congress Catalog Card Number: 96-60923

*Page 1: Simple planting in unusual containers, such as these cone-shaped wicker baskets, successfully
breaks up a dull expanse of fence or wall.*

Pages 2–3: The assortment of containers and plants lining this path brings a welcome burst of color.

*Page 5: The light and airy conditions offered by a balcony are ideal for growing trailing plants and fruits. Even a small
planter will yield a generous crop of strawberries.*

Contents

Introduction 7

Materials and Methods 9

Planting Design 21

Pots 31

Hanging Baskets 53

Windowboxes 67

Plant Directory 81

Index 94

Acknowledgments 96

Introduction

Container gardening is, above all, about flexibility: whether you are gardening in vast acres or on the tiniest of balconies, containers give you the opportunity to introduce color, shape, and texture wherever and whenever they are needed.

All the practical information you will need to create and sustain container planting schemes is given here. Armed with this essential knowledge, you will have the confidence to design your own displays, match plants to containers, and place them to best advantage. Appearing at intervals throughout the book is a range of original planting schemes, set out as easy-to-follow practical projects, showing how pots, hanging baskets, and windowboxes, as well as improvised containers, can be used to exciting and dramatic effect.

The extensive directory contains all the essential information you will need for the care and cultivation of over 150 plants. It will also encourage you to experiment with more unusual plants, to create your own original container displays.

Containers of colorful flowers can be used to create unexpected surprises in dark corners of the garden. Here, the shadowy background serves to emphasize the brightness of the pelargoniums and felicias as they are caught by the sun's rays.

Whatever container you choose, whether a custom-made terracotta windowbox or a chipped enamel bucket, a reproduction stone urn, wire hanging basket, or an old wooden feeding trough, each has its own advantages and disadvantages. This chapter looks at the best uses of all these materials, helping you to make the most of their special characteristics and thereby enabling you to explore the enormous scope of container gardening. It then examines the huge range of plants you can consider, before supplying all the practical information you will need on potting soils, drainage, watering, and feeding, to ensure that your plants remain healthy and vigorous throughout the growing season.

Materials and Methods

ABOVE: *New terracotta is the perfect surface for painting colorful patterns in latex or oil-based paint.*
LEFT: *Good quality potting soil, whether soilless or soil-based, will provide the right conditions for strong root growth and healthy container plants.*

TYPES OF CONTAINER

Plant containers come in a wide range of styles and materials, from grand stone urns to earthy hand-thrown terracotta ware, from plain plastic pots to glazed ceramic jars. Inventive gardeners will see potential in all sorts of unlikely objects— an old coal bucket, a washtub, a shiny new trash can, or a kitchen colander.

Every material has its virtues, and, as long as it provides good growing conditions, even the most undistinguished-looking container can be planted or decorated to make a big impact. The simplest decorative techniques will transform the humblest of containers—painting, stenciling, or gilding, binding with rope, covering with shells, or creating patterns with mosaic tesserae.

TERRACOTTA

Terracotta is a natural material that provides good growing conditions. The porous clay helps to prevent the potting soil becoming waterlogged and allows air to the roots, while evaporation from the pot helps to keep the roots cool, although this increases the need for watering.

Terracotta is prone to frost damage, so minimize the risk by keeping the potting soil well drained. Ask whether the pot is frostproof when you buy it.

Although new terracotta can look stark, it will develop a patina. Machine-made pots take longer than hand-thrown ones to do this, but you can accelerate the ageing process by keeping empty pots in a damp, shady place to encourage the growth of greenery, or by painting them with sour milk or plain yogurt.

Broken pots can be repaired with adhesive, but, to be more traditional, you can drill a line of holes down each side of the break with a masonry drill, and then tie wire across the break at each matching pair of holes, giving a scar-like effect.

PLASTIC

Plastic containers are inexpensive and come in a wide variety of colors, shapes, and styles. Non-porous plastic keeps potting soil moist for longer than terracotta, and generally the planting itself shades the container and protects the roots from heat damage. Plastic pots can usually be lifted and moved easily if they are filled with peat moss potting soil but this leaves the pots less stable.

WOOD

Wooden containers are especially good for insulating roots from extremes of temperature. You can make your own using either pressure-treated or planed wood, but the latter will need painting or treating with a plant-friendly preservative. An annual coat of quality car wax will also help prolong their life. You may need to drill drainage holes or use a durable liner inside to prevent the wet potting soil rotting the wood.

ABOVE: *Olive oil cans, with a simple, complementary planting of* Petunia "Brass Band," *make cheap and colorful improvised containers.*
FAR LEFT: *Terracotta pots come in various shapes and sizes, suiting many styles of planting.*

STONE

Stone troughs exude a sense of timeless stability. More elaborate urns, meanwhile, tend to be used more selfconsciously as decorative focal points. Reconstructed stone is a cheaper alternative to natural stone, and its starkness will weather down—relatively quickly if you treat the surface.

METAL

Painted or left untreated, and planted with strong foliage, metal containers work well in modern, clean-lined gardens, and can add a whimsical touch in a traditional setting. Try battered old buckets and troughs as well as shiny new ones.

Plants for Containers

Almost all types of garden plant can be grown in containers—shrubs, climbers, hardy and tender perennials, annuals, bulbs, alpines, grasses, fruits, vegetables, and herbs. Certain houseplants and succulents also enjoy a summer outdoors, and will provide good foliage to mix with bedding plants in a container.

In fact, container gardening has positive advantages. You can create displays that might be difficult or impossible in a border by grouping plants with different soil requirements in a series

Evergreen box make impressive container plants. Large, established specimens need regular feeding.

of pots. In addition, certain tender plants that would not survive the winter in a border will thrive in pots since they can be moved indoors or to a warmer, sheltered part of the garden.

Container plantings will be more exciting and original if you include some out-of-the-ordinary plants; you can track them down in *The Anderson Horticultural Library's Source List of Plants and Seeds*, which offers a comprehensive listing of thousands of plants and the nurseries that stock them. Or visit horticultural shows where specialist growers exhibit and sell new plant specimens.

Experiment with your plantings, too. Do not be put off because you are not sure if a combination will work. If you use your common sense and avoid trying to combine opposing extremes, such as sun-loving plants and those that prefer damp conditions, you will create some exciting and dramatic displays.

SHRUBS

In a large container planting, shrubs can either stand dramatically alone or create a permanent framework around which seasonal interest can be introduced—through perennials, bulbs, and annuals. Evergreen shrubs obviously make a year-round contribution, but there are many deciduous shrubs with attractive foliage or stem color, or an interesting outline shape, that are invaluable for introducing some sort of seasonal variety.

PERENNIALS

Summer-flowering tender perennials, such as osteospermums, pelargoniums, and gazanias, are an essential ingredient of container plantings. With their long flowering season, they are invaluable for creating an effect of abundance, and are the mainstay of small pots, hanging baskets, and windowboxes alike. The terrific range of colors they offer gives scope for some dramatic designs. If it is not possible to overwinter them in a conservatory or heated greenhouse (see page 19), you must decide whether to take cuttings to grow on, leave them out and risk the weather, or discard them as annuals.

Hardy perennials do not need winter protection, and will provide interest throughout the growing season—not only with flowers. If planted in fall or winter, they will signal spring's arrival with colorful new buds of foliage. The emergent growth of euphorbias, peonies, and ferns has an intensity of texture and hue probably unmatched in any mature foliage.

Easily grown but tender, sedges make striking architectural displays. Simple, unembellished pots enhance their qualities.

ABOVE: *Exotic fruits, such as lemons, give a distinctive hot-climate feel to a garden.*
FAR RIGHT: *Tulips, available in colors across the spectrum, are among the showiest of bulbs, and create a vibrant, late spring display.*

As a hardy plant's flowering season is brief compared with that of a tender perennial, it needs to have good foliage in order to be equally effective in and out of flower. Hostas, with their distinctively shaped, variegated or textured leaves,

are an obvious choice. Combined with grasses such as *Molinia caerulea* "Variegata" or *Helichtotrichon sempervirens*, they have considerable impact.

ANNUALS

Annuals are an inexpensive and easy way to produce an abundance of color. Modern hybrids have been bred to produce weatherproof and free-flowering plants. Keep an eye out for unusual subjects in seed catalogs, and give them a try.

BULBS

Many bulbs fare better in the sharply drained conditions that pot culture allows than in cold, damp soils. They provide both vibrant color and a selection of bold and often unusual flower and leaf shapes. Underplanting with bulbs can extend the season of winter plantings, and, with careful planning, your display might last from mid-winter to late spring. Beware of using tulips in a winter display that is to be replanted with summer flowers because many tulips are in full flower just when you want to change the planting; use separate pots instead for the tulips and let them flower right through. Feed all spring-flowering bulbs regularly until the leaves die back if you want to keep them for the following year.

DROUGHT-TOLERANT PLANTS

Given the neglect often suffered by plants in containers, drought-tolerant plants make sensible choices, particularly for patios and courtyards, which tend to be sun traps. Use succulents and Mediterranean plants such as *Myrtus communis* (myrtle), *Phlomis fruticosa* (Jerusalem sage), and herbs, which adapt well to hot, dry conditions.

PRACTICAL PLANTING

Over and above ensuring that your plants are provided with the basic growing requirements—light, water, and potting soil—successful container planting is largely trial and error. You must observe and analyze the performance of your plants throughout the season, familiarizing yourself with their individual needs in order to acquire the best possible understanding of them—knowledge that will give you the confidence to grow an ever-increasing variety.

POTTING SOILS

There are essentially two types of growing medium: soil-based and soilless potting soils.

Traditionally, soil-based potting soils contain a mixture of sand, loam, and fertilizers. They are inherently fertile, releasing their nutrients over a period of time, making them ideally suited to long-term container plantings. Readily rewetted when they become dry, soil-based potting soils are heavy, which is a disadvantage if you want to move pots around, but an advantage if you have a large or top-heavy planting that is likely to blow over and needs stabilizing. Soil-based potting soils usually contain lime, so they are not suitable for acid-loving plants, which should be grown in an ericaceous (or acidic) potting soil.

Soilless potting soils were traditionally peat moss-based, but in response to ecologicial concerns about the depletion of peat bogs, they are now made from a variety of materials, including bark and cocoa shells. With no natural nutritional value, all nutrients have to be added, and plants grown in soilless potting soil need feeding through the season. They are light and easy to handle, however, and combine good water retention with good aeration, provided that the soil is not firmed too much when the containers are planted.

Never pot plants in garden soil. Not only do you risk importing weed seeds, soil pests, and diseases, you are likely to end up with a solid mass of earth that neither water nor air can penetrate.

FEEDING

Nutrients can either be incorporated in the potting soil before you add your plants, or added later as liquid feed. Slow-release fertilizers, in the

Slow-release fertilizer added to soil-based
potting soil prolongs its life for another season.

form of granules, provide soilless potting soils with enough nutrients to last the duration of a whole growing season.

Traditional organic equivalents of the slow-release fertilizer are hoof and horn, and bonemeal. Hoof and horn releases nitrogen steadily over a long period, for leafy growth, while bonemeal provides phosphate to stimulate root growth. It can make potting soils alkaline, however, so do not use it with lime-hating plants like rhododendrons and camellias.

Liquid feeding involves adding plant food to the water at intervals during the growing season. Never add more feed to get a bigger, better plant: too much fertilizer prevents water uptake and the plant may wilt even when the compost is wet.

For quick, if short-lived, results either use a foliar feed that is sprayed directly onto the leaves, or water an ammonium sulfate solution (1oz to the gallon) onto damp potting soil, avoiding contact with the foliage. Both supply a nitrogen boost, stimulating lush, green growth.

WATERING

Plant roots need a balance of air and water. Both underwatering and overwatering can upset this balance and cause the plants to suffer. Dry, soilless potting soils can be difficult to rewet because once the soil shrinks and cracks, the water simply runs straight through. Either immerse the container in a bowl of water and soak it for half an hour, or add dishwashing liquid to the watering can. This will help the peat moss to absorb the water. Too regular a use of detergent will deplete the soil's oxygen, so be careful. Meanwhile, the surface of a soil-based potting soil will, over time, become compacted and crusted with watering, making it equally inefficient as a means of transport for water and air. A layer of organic mulch such as peat moss, bark, or cocoa shells on the soil's surface will prevent this.

It is easy to assume that pots will not need watering after a good downpour, but foliage can prevent the rain reaching the potting soil. However, you should certainly collect and use your rainwater, particularly in hard-water areas, where lime from tap water can build up in the soil, making it unsuitable for lime-hating plants. Although you can add granules of chelated iron to the water to alleviate the problem, prevention is always better than cure.

Most plants should be watered thoroughly, and then left to dry out slightly before being watered again. The most effective method is to pour water gently into the base of a planting—without using a rose. Avoid always watering in the same place, because this can damage the foliage, creating a "hole" in the display. To reach hanging baskets or awkwardly positioned pots, tie a garden cane to the hose in order to stiffen the end and give you more control.

Always soak plants well before planting them. Since the roots will not penetrate the new potting soil for a week or two, it is very important to ensure that water reaches them and not just the surrounding soil.

You can now buy polymer gels to mix into a potting soil to improve its water-retentive capacity, thereby reducing the amount of watering required. The crystals absorb water and swell up to many times their size to form a water reservoir for the plant roots.

This temporary watering system uses strips of disposable kitchen cloth. Move your pots into the shade and out of the wind and place a bucket of water at a level above the pots. From this lead lengths of cloth to each pot and peg them into the compost. Capillary action will siphon a slow trickle of water along the cloth to the pots.

Regular repotting encourages a healthy and vigorous root system, which will rapidly send roots into the potting soil when planted out.

If you have lots of containers, it may be worth considering an automatic watering device. Systems consist of narrow, connecting pipes that are clipped into individual containers, and watering is regulated by a time switch on the garden faucet. Controlling the amount of water required and the timing is difficult since container size, plant size, and variations in the weather make accurate calculation impossible. A system that uses a moisture-sensitive device pushed into the potting soil will make the most economic use of water. In hard water areas, lime deposits may block the ends of the drip pipes, so you should check them regularly.

DRAINAGE

Good drainage is vital since too much water in the potting soil drives out the air and kills the roots. For that reason, you should never leave pots standing in saucers of water.

Plants and bulbs left sitting in wet potting soil may suffer root-rot, and containers full of sodden soil are more likely to crack in a frost. Sit containers on a porous, free-draining surface, such as gravel, or use terracotta feet or a wedge to allow any excess water to drain away.

Broken crocks are often placed in the bottom of a pot to assist drainage. This is not necessary if some of the soil is touching whatever the pot is sitting on. If the container is raised off the ground, however, you will need a layer of gravel or crocks to act as a sump.

POTTING AND REPOTTING

When selecting container plants, consider their mature dimensions, but remember that a plant in a pot has a restricted root zone and so its growth will be limited. Use a container in which a root system sufficiently large to support the plant can develop, or carefully prune the plant to make it smaller and more manageable.

It is generally advisable to renew the soil every year or two—in late winter or early spring when the plants are dormant. Water the day before repotting: a moist rootball will come out more easily than a dry one. Trim off any visible roots to make it easier to get the rootball out intact. Shake out or wash off some of the soil from the roots, and prune out up to a quarter of them if they are congested as new roots will grow into the fresh soil. Place the plant in its new pot and feed soil around the roots. Use a stick to prod soil into the spaces between the roots, and gently shake the plant as you fill the pot with soil. You may need to top up the soil after one or two waterings.

For a dense planting, you will need a good volume of potting soil—for stability as well as moisture and nutrition—so deeper, wider containers are best.

DEADHEADING

Regular deadheading will keep a planting scheme fresh and encourage new flower buds. Cutting off dead leaves with hand pruners or scissors takes very little time, and, as well as keeping displays tidy, helps prevent infection.

SURVIVING THE WINTER

A wide range of exotic plants can be grown in containers, and some will stand a few degrees of frost as long as they are kept almost dry. However, many need to be moved from the garden during the winter months. In exceptionally cold snaps, horticultural blankets, close-woven nylon mesh, or newspaper wrapped around tender plants will help protect their leaves.

A temperature just above freezing in a small greenhouse, outhouse, or conservatory will see this tender bougainvillea through the winter.

PERHAPS THE MOST EXCITING aspect of designing with plants is the knowledge that the design is only the start: plants will grow into each other in ways that you can never predict. While both the shape of your container and its location may be limiting factors, there is still fantastic scope for imaginative designs, given the incredible variety of plant shapes and habits, flower and foliage colors available. But how do you ensure your plantings achieve a delicate balance, and that the overall effect doesn't smother the details of individual plants? In looking at combinations of plants in single containers, and combinations of containers in a variety of settings, this chapter will help you to plan successful displays.

Planting Design

ABOVE: *The broad, woolly leaves of Salvia argentea and the fine leaves of the grass illustrate the value of contrasting foliage textures, shapes, and colors.*
LEFT: *Clashing colors can create vibrant displays. Here, orange lilies do battle with purple salvias.*

CREATIVE PLANTING

Choosing plants that are arresting or unusual is one method of creating a distinctive planting. Another is to use common plants in unusual ways, such as hostas in hanging baskets or succulents among lush foliage. With a well-drained potting soil and reasonably light and airy conditions, you will be able to grow a surprising mixture of plants in the same pot. The art of combining plants lies in using their shapes and colors to contribute to the overall effect, while allowing each plant to retain its own identity.

USING SHAPES

Including plants with a well-defined shape—whether bushy, spiky, or arching—will always simplify the process of creating a successful planting. Long-term plantings need a good structure to underpin the more transient, surface layer of flower color. Plants with bold, upright leaves, or arching or trailing stems will help build and define the structure.

Plants with simple, large leaves have a stabilizing effect. Used at the bottom of a group of plants, they create a strong base. Architectural

plants such as melianthus and hedychiums lend themselves to more dramatic arrangements; they have a stately look, which is easily softened by smaller, lighter plants. Single specimens can take the place of ornaments in the garden.

A sense of summer is evoked by using small-leaved flowering plants to create a wispy, "frizzy" look. But take care not to let a soft, unchallenging planting lose its character or become indistinct. Large, plain leaves will soothe a planting, while spiky and finely cut leaves can jazz it up.

Flowers with distinctive shapes, like abutilons and agapanthus, can bring emphasis to a planting. The number of flowers on a plant and the way they are presented is just as important. The many upright stems of lilac flowers borne by *Nemesia fruticans* create an effect that is as useful as the arching stems and tiny flowerheads of many grasses.

Nevertheless it is a plant's leaves that have to sustain the display as the flowers come and go around them. It is not difficult to make striking associations with foliage alone, given the astonishing diversity of leaf shape and texture: not just large or small, but huge or tiny, rounded, pointed, ribbed, glossy, or furry. A simple but effective rule is always to place plants with dissimilar foliage in adjacent containers, so that each is brought into relief by the other—hostas beside bamboo, for instance.

LEFT: *Foliage plants form the basis of this design, with flowering plants added to introduce color and unify the arrangement.*
RIGHT: *The combination of gray and purple foliage links this container planting with the border plants in a masterly way.*

The same is true within a planting. Strong plants can combine to form an indistinct planting because their flowers and foliage are too similar, but if you introduce a third, which creates a series of contrasts in shape and texture, all three plants begin to benefit from their association, and the planting immediately acquires more character.

USING COLOR

The gardener's palette is every bit as extensive as the painter's. Flowers and foliage alike exhibit a startling array of colors, so selecting a particular color scheme for a planting will allow you to concentrate on a smaller group of plants and exploit them fully. It will also help to make one planting distinct from another.

While some people have a natural eye for color, others need guidance and inspiration. You could take the color of your container as a starting point. Terracotta pots look particularly good filled with warm oranges and reds, for example, while the smooth coolness of an old lead container or a copper cistern patterned with verdigris suggests plants with a metallic look—the blues and grays of the heavily silvered cultivars of *Begonia rex*, steely blue grasses, blue-gray succulent echeverias, or *Correa backhouseana*, with blue-green leaves and pale yellow flowers. The same containers luxuriantly planted with pure white and primrose-yellow flowers (*Coreopsis verticillata* "Moonbeam" would be perfect) have a brighter, softer look that is just as attractive.

The contrasting colors and shapes of agapanthus, Phygelius aequalis "Yellow Trumpet," hebe, and sempervivum lead the eye around this display.

Use a paint color chart to see what color container works best with your plants. Dark green is always safe, but the impact will be greater if you experiment. Either paint your pots in cheerful colors that contrast well with the planting, or try to match or tone them with your plants.

Always consider where the container is to be placed. If it is on a patio near the house, think how particular colors will relate to the paintwork of the house or the patio furniture. If it is near a border, the scheme should harmonize with the colors in that border; use some of the same flowers in both and make an echo. Color links will give your designs purpose, drawing disparate parts of a garden together.

Colors can be combined to create specific moods: yellow with purple is lively; red with orange and yellow, found ready-blended in the nasturtium, is warm and cheerful; when blue and purple are mixed, the mood is more subdued. Combining any blue, gray, pink, or purple plants will create a soft, harmonious effect. Primrose-yellow will complement any of these colors, all of which are found in the leaves of many good foliage plants, as well as in flowers.

Lime-green is stunning mixed with orange, particularly if the orange is pale, and more yellow than red. Blue and red both tend to distract the eye, but reds with an element of blue in them work with purple to give a rich, regal feel. Purple and gray foliage makes a somber but distinguished arrangement. White works well in any color scheme, while green should never be underestimated. Not only will it give definition to bright flowers, but it will also add depth to an arrangement that would otherwise appear as a solid mass of color. There is only one golden rule of color that needs to be observed: do not mix reds from the blue end of the spectrum with reds from the yellow end, for example fuchsias with orange marigolds, and violet petunias with orange-red nasturtiums.

The soft yellows and oranges of abutilons and **Begonia sutherlandii** *harmonize with the table and chairs. The purple petunias prevent the arrangement from becoming too contrived.*

USING CONTAINERS

There are many different ways of incorporating containers in a garden design: clustered together, in repetitive rows, individually, worked into borders, hanging from trees or pergolas, perched on windowsills or walls—only your imagination limits you. However, it is important to match plants with appropriate containers, and to relate your planting style to the style of your garden.

The inspiration for container plantings may come from a particular part of the garden that you want to decorate and from the feeling or effect you wish to create there. You need to consider how the background will influence the design as you plan: whether the plants will be seen against a wall, a fence, evergreen hedging, or larger shrubs in a border. The dark, architectural leaves of

Phormium tenax "Purpureum" will lose much of their strength against dark brick, but will stand out clearly against a busy border. Tall, large-leaved plants, such as hedychiums or zantedeschias, will also help to disguise unattractive backgrounds.

Often the only way to grow plants in small, paved gardens or courtyards or roof gardens is in containers. You can even arrange pots of hardy perennials to resemble a border, moving the plants to the back of the display as they go over.

In every garden there are small microclimates that can be exploited to grow a greater assortment of plants. The spot between the garden wall and the house might be one or two degrees warmer than elsewhere because it gets heat from the house and is sheltered from the wind, so you can grow exotics, such as passion flower and myrtle, without protection. If it has a sunny aspect, you will also be able to exploit the winter sunshine.

It will be cooler and shadier under a tree in summer, but on clear winter nights the branches can also help reduce heat loss from the ground, thereby diminishing the effect of frost.

FORMAL PLANTINGS

The term "formal garden" probably conjures up images of parterres, knot gardens, and grand designs on a large scale, but in fact small gardens lend themselves very readily to formal arrangements. Formality relies for its effect on balance and repetition. To create a look that is strictly formal, use identical containers in rows, each planted with the same type and shape of plant.

The traditional choice for formal planting is evergreen box or yew, clipped into regular shapes. Holly and bay can be grown as standards, although

FAR LEFT: *This witty trio of dwarf sunflowers in terracotta pots lifts the spirits and brightens up the dull brick wall behind.*

LEFT: *This row of repeated box spirals is formal but modern looking. The irregularity of the top shelf emphasizes the regimented display on the bottom shelves. Clipping box requires patience, but results such as this are well worth the effort.*

ABOVE: *Boldly colored pansies in traditional terracotta pots on an ornamental shelf make a simple yet elegant composition.*

bay will suffer in a cold winter. In a paved garden, set standard plants in rows to make the most of the dramatic shadows they cast, or use their shadows to break up bare areas of wall by placing the containers a little way out from the wall.

A pair of containers, one either side of a doorway, or small pots flanking a flight of steps, create a pleasing symmetry that adds formality to a garden. If the planting is complicated, the container has to be simple with a strong shape to maintain the formal look. Large terracotta pots and Versailles tubs are ideal.

Snow and frost lying on pots arranged in geometric patterns have a striking effect. In summer, on the other hand, you can lighten a formal scheme without detracting from its strength by introducing flowering plants with a single color scheme.

ABOVE: *A niche cut into the dense foliage of a hornbeam hedge makes a novel setting for a pot of variegated pelargoniums, echeverias, and ivy.*
ABOVE RIGHT: *The lush foliage of bamboos, dahlias, salvias, and hedychiums can turn a dull backyard into a wonderful jumble of greenery.*

BACKYARD JUNGLES

By choosing a mixture of hardy and tender exotic-looking plants, you can create a jungle in containers outside your back door. Use tall, large-leaved plants such as *Paulownia tomentosa*, *Aralia elata*, and *Gunnera chilensis* crowded together to produce a lush, tropical atmosphere. Give these plants as big a root-run as possible to support their exuberant growth; use large containers, and feed the plants well. Place showy flowers like cannas, tigridias, *Incarvillea delavayi*, and *Vallota speciosa* among them.

ROOF GARDENS

If you live in a top-floor apartment and have access to a strong, flat roof, you can use containers to create a roof garden.

Although a roof garden has the advantage of increased natural light, it is a harsh environment exposed to wind and sun. You can erect trellis windbreaks or use the existing chimney stacks or air-conditioning units as shelter to alleviate the ill effects, and choosing plants suited to dry conditions will help. Use a soil-based potting soil, but beware the extra weight.

Unless there is a barrier around the perimeter, you should secure any pots to prevent them being blown over the edge. Wires stretched between vine eyes, drilled and plugged into any available brickwork, will support climbing plants; the pots themselves could, if necessary, be fixed to them.

CONTAINERS IN BORDERS

Pots nestling in borders so that they are not immediately obvious are like treasures waiting to be found. Stand your pots on clay pipes or stout logs, or set them on a tile or slab to imitate Roman columns with flowerpot "busts"—very effective if repeated along the whole border.

Containers allow you to fill seasonal gaps in borders or make quick alterations to a planting scheme.

POTS ON WALLS, POTS IN BORDERS, pots in rows, pots on shelves: pots of all shapes and sizes can be carefully arranged in pairs or patterns, or grouped more informally to produce a dramatically different effect every time. Big pots make a big impression, whether planted or empty, but you can make an even bigger one by choosing a large, bold plant with a strong shape as the centerpiece of a grand planting. Collections of small pots, on the other hand, can be used to create a particular theme or color scheme, even a special mood, in a corner of the garden. Portable, versatile, and low-maintenance, and capable of providing the garden with great visual excitement, pots offer the imaginative gardener huge scope.

Pots

ABOVE: *Large, ornate pots can become the focus of a garden room. A planting without the distraction of flowers allows your attention to rest on the container.*
LEFT: *A tiered display of plants invites you to peer closely at the different shapes, colors, and textures.*

TYPES OF POT

Pots are available in all shapes and sizes, styles and materials, to suit every kind of garden, whether traditional or modern, formal or informal. If you want to add an individual touch to your planting displays, it is easy to improvise your own pots from recycled household objects.

FLOWERPOTS

The traditional terracotta flowerpot is relatively inexpensive, unbeatably versatile, and available in a vast array of sizes, ranging from 1 inch to over 3 feet in diameter. Its simple shape makes it ideal for multi-pot displays. Plastic flowerpots are cheaper, but less attractive.

PEDESTAL URNS

Pedestal urns have an elegance of proportion that is perfect for formal settings, and which can be enhanced by giving the planting enough height in the center to balance the height of the pedestal.

Because they hold only a relatively small amount of potting soil, however, plants near the rim of the urn tend to dry out rather quickly.

VERSAILLES TUBS

Basically square, wooden boxes with feet, these are ideal in formal settings planted with individual standard trees and topiary shapes. They are well suited to long-term planting because they hold a large volume of potting soil.

LOW, FLAT CONTAINERS

Giving a stable and solid look, this shape works particularly well on paved areas around garden benches where the height of the container is in scale with the seated gardener. Low, squat pots work equally well whether alone or grouped with taller pots. Plants such as tradescantias, *Senecio viravira*, *Bidens ferulifolia*, *Anthemis punctata cupaniana*, *Plectranthus* species, and nasturtiums will trail over the edge and along the ground to maintain this horizontal bias.

BULBOUS POTS

In the right position, an empty bulbous pot left on its side makes a useful ornament. But its shape is particularly well suited to full, informal planting, with *Helichrysum petiolare* and *Diascia vigilis* spilling out and down its sides. Placing one amid a group of straight-sided pots creates a pleasing

LEFT: *Painted wooden containers of clipped box are ideally suited to formal, geometric designs.*
ABOVE RIGHT: *A planting should always be in proportion to the shape and size of its pot. These tall tulips are of just the right size and scale.*

effect, too. But there are problems: it is all but impossible to remove large plants for repotting, and, when the potting soil freezes, round-bellied, narrow-necked pots are prone to crack.

WALL POTS

Wall pots come in wire, terracotta, plastic, and wicker, but you can just as easily use old paint cans. Hang the pots with nails, or use hooks or screws; drill or plug them into the chosen surface.

Wall pots look equally good with a formal or informal planting. A striking effect can be created by planting rows of pots with the same luxuriant scheme, so that the plants spill out and hide the pots completely. Remember that wall pots are usually small, and are often out of the rain under the eaves, so they tend to dry out quickly.

IMPROVISED POTS

Anything that will hold potting soil and allow excess water to drain away is a potential plant container. Kitchens, garden sheds, and attics are all worth exploring for novel receptacles ready for a new life: old colanders, cake pans, vegetable baskets, buckets, fruit boxes, tea chests, sinks, milk churns, wire and wicker baskets will all make new dramatic settings for plants. Be adventurous, and you will create a highly original focal point.

USING POTS

Just as ornaments can stamp an owner's personality on a house, so small pots can personalize a garden, whether placed singly or in groups. Collections of small pots can "busy up" dull corners, and they are ideal for visually breaking up large expanses of bare wall or paving.

Small container plantings offer great creative scope for playing with different colors, textures, and forms. The mix and range of plants can be

Each pot within a display should have a character of its own. Here, **Lagurus ovatus** *and white lobelia combine to create an interesting cameo within a large arrangement.*

easily altered, and pots rearranged, to suit the changing seasons or to create different moods. Flower colors can range across the whole spectrum, while pots of large-leaved plants such as hostas can be placed close by to act as foils for the bright colors.

A collection of evergreen sempervivums creates a textured pattern of subdued colors and needs only the minimum of attention. When planted singly in pots, or in groups in flat pans, they soon grow to make a mosaic of densely packed rosettes. Neat and compact, these plants are suitable for even the tiniest of containers.

While large pots must be positioned with care to make the greatest impact, there are fewer restrictions governing the placement of small pots. Arranging containers at different heights allows each plant to display its distinct qualities. Simple plantings of a single species placed in lines can be used instead of fences to mark off different areas of the garden.

Large pots allow the gardener to create lavish, bold designs. They lend themselves to large plants with striking leaves and vigorous growth. While still acting as a complement to the garden planting as a whole, these containers will stand in their own right, and, if they contain shrubs or other long-term plants, can be adapted to provide a year-round display. Think of them as you would a piece of garden sculpture, and position them where they will make striking focal points. Large pots can be used to dramatic effect on roof terraces or balconies, since their size is more imposing in a confined space, but first check that these areas can actually support the weight of the planted container.

ABOVE: *In time, the* Acaena *"Glauca,"* Ajuga reptans *"Atropurpurea,"* Lysimachia nummularia, *and euonymus in this pot will grow into the border.*

LEFT: *Massing small pots around a larger one creates a richness to compare with a garden border.*

DESIGNING SCHEMES

A planting scheme starts to change the moment you create it, and will not reach its full glory until many weeks later. Any planting that is to include a number of different types of plant has an element of unpredictability about it, and a big problem for the novice container gardener is knowing how different plants will behave together. What looks to be a nicely balanced planting at the beginning of the season can turn into a lopsided jungle by the end because the original sizes of the plants bear no relation to their eventual heights. Find out as much as you can about about the growth rate and mature size of unfamiliar plants before you start. But remember that a pot-confined plant will grow more slowly than one in the ground.

Use a plant with plenty of character at the center of a large pot to give structure to the group, and to form the body or bulk of the finished planting: melianthus, miscanthus, and daturas are good plants for this purpose. Around this central axis, arrange other plants that will complement or contrast, and then add finer, softer foliage plants, such as *Lavatera maritima* and *Lotus hirsutus*, which can be tucked in among these large leaves. The contrast of large leaves with fine leaves, and soft, furry leaves with hard,

shiny leaves will not create the confusing effect you might expect. Flowers will soften the planting scheme, as well as adding to the color and richness of the composition.

Trailing plants can be used around the edges to spill attractively over the sides of the pot, and, mixed in with the main planting, to create strong horizontal or arching lines; *Helichrysum petiolare* is ideal. *Glechoma hederacea* will give a decisive vertical line to the edge of a planting. Lobelias, bacopas, and diascias give a bushy, more luxuriant look, whereas *Felicia petiolata* and *Plectranthus coleoides* "Variegatus" arch out gracefully.

Stand back and look at the arrangement as you build it, and ask yourself questions: Where is the interest? Why am I putting this here? Do I need something tall and graceful, or short and squat?

MONOCHROMATIC PLANTINGS

Although often used for miniature alpine gardens, old-fashioned, white ceramic sinks can be planted in more striking ways: one idea is to use a monochromatic color scheme to offset the harsh texture and color of the sink. A base planting of the black *Ophiopogon planiscapus* "Nigrescens" might be combined with white hyacinths for the spring and replaced by white *Felicia amelloides* "Read's White" and white petunias in the summer. A mulch of black marble chippings will stop the potting soil splashing onto the glaze, and also tie in with the color scheme.

LEFT: *Simple color schemes can be very effective, particularly in large-scale plantings.*
RIGHT: **Verbena bonariensis** *tumbles to the ground in this informal scheme of pink and white.*

In winter, when flowers are in short supply, plants with strong architectural shapes, such as yuccas, take on extra importance.

DRY PLANTINGS

Mediterranean plants, such as *Teucrium fruticans* (shrubby germander), *Coronilla glauca, Lotus hirsutus, Phlomis fruticosa* (Jerusalem sage), myrtle, and rosemary, make strong and characterful mixed summer plantings for small and large pots alike. They all enjoy hot, dry conditions, which is ideal as containers tend to get very dry in summer. You can develop the Mediterranean theme: trailing succulents such as *Ceropegia woodii* and *Lotus berthelotii* will add another dimension, while stones, pebbles, bleached driftwood, and grit to mulch the top of pots will emphasize the feeling of dryness.

Otherwise, extend the season of interest with bulbs that are happy in pots and whose flowers or leaves suit the dry look—*Nectaroscordum siculum bulgaricum,* for instance, or *Allium christophii.* The blue-tinged leaves and soft apricot flowers of the short *Tulipa batalinii* will both complement late spring plantings and appreciate a hot baking in the summer. A plant like *Vallota speciosa* (Scarborough lily) will finish the season showily.

WINTER PLANTINGS

For winter schemes, use a container that is both frostproof and rustproof. Choose your plants carefully—creative winter planting presents a real challenge since the main interest must come from the foliage of evergreen shrubs. There are a variety of suitable evergreens, such as holly, box, yew, *Osmanthus delavayi, O. heterophyllus,* and *Prunus lusitanica.* Because growth is slow during the winter, these plants can be left in their own pots and plunged into a larger container. Use a single species of plant, like box, or mix two or more plants—yew with osmanthus, say—to emphasize the foliage of each. Underplant with evergreen ferns such as *Polypodium vulgare* and dryopteris for another layer of interest.

You need to choose a shrub for the center of the pot that tolerates annual pruning in order to maintain the scale and balance of the design.

Plants with colored stems, such as *Cornus stolonifera* "Flaviramea" (yellow-green) or *Salix alba* "Britzensis" (glowing orange), add a welcome lightness, while ivies trailed over the edge will help to lessen the slightly stiff look of many evergreens. The fresh greenery of wallflowers can be used to fill any gaps in a winter arrangement and then you can enjoy their richly colored, scented flowers in the spring, while underplanting with bulbs—snowdrops and the smaller daffodils—will also bring rewards as the year unfolds.

MAINTENANCE

All container plantings will require maintenance to keep them looking at their best (see pages 16–19), but there are certain tasks that apply particularly to plantings in pots.

No matter how carefully you choose your plants, some will not grow as you originally envisaged. By keeping an eye on the planting as it develops and adjusting it as necessary, the different plants will stay in proportion to each other and their pot. Cut back the shoots of a larger-leaved plant to a healthy-looking bud farther down the stem if it starts to smother its smaller neighbors; careful pruning will maintain a balance between the two.

Some plants will need support. A cane pushed right through the root ball and as far into the potting soil as possible will prevent a top-heavy standard breaking in the wind. Tall species, like abutilons and standard fuchsias, can be tied to a

An improvised pot made from vine prunings, intertwined and lined with moss, makes a light and free-draining container.

cane with soft string, while some plants that would normally trail, such as *Helichrysum petiolare*, can be trained up a cane to produce an airy, tiered effect. You can also create an attractive feature by pushing willow stems around the edge of your container and tying them at the top to make a wigwam for climbing plants to use—clematis, jasmine, and honeysuckle will happily oblige.

PROJECT: *CLASS GLASS*

this a thin layer of sand. (Run the grit and sand in through a funnel to keep the glass clean.) Cut out a coffee filter paper to the shape of the vase, and place it on top of the sand. Place one festuca in the vase so you can judge how much potting soil you will need.

3 Remove the plant and add the required amount of potting soil. Insert the two festucas. Tease a well-rooted shoot of ophiopogon from the parent plant, and place it between the festucas. Carefully fill around them with soil.

FOLIAGE PLANTS and colored layers of potting soil, sand, stones, and grit are here blended into a startling piece of art.

INGREDIENTS
Glass vase
Horticultural grit
Granite chippings
Play sand
Funnel
Coffee filter paper
Soilless potting soil
(Clay pebbles, perlite, and charcoal can also be used to create different-colored layers)
PLANTS
Festuca glauca "Silver Sea" x 2
Ophiopogon planiscapus
   "Nigrescens" x 1

1 Assemble the plants and materials. Water the plants well, but keep the other ingredients as dry as possible.

2 Line the base of the vase with 1½–2 inches of horticultural grit. Add a 2-inch layer of granite chippings, and on top of

RIGHT: *The finished project displayed on a conservatory shelf with* Artemisia *"Powis Castle,"* Pelargonium *"The Crocodile," and* Euphorbia cyparissias.

PROJECT: *BEYOND THE PAIL*

ALL SORTS OF HOUSEHOLD ITEMS can be adapted to make effective improvised containers. A zinc bucket, with holes drilled into the base for drainage, becomes a robust and stable pot for this tall planting of jasmine. Willow stems act as a support.

INGREDIENTS AND TOOLS
Zinc bucket
Electric drill
Gravel
Soil-based potting soil
Long willow shoots x 4
String
PLANTS
Jasminum polyanthum x 2

1 Gather together the materials and plants. Make sure the plants are well watered.

2 Turn the bucket upside down, and drill a series of large drainage holes in the base.

3 Cover the bottom of the bucket with 1¼–2 inches of gravel, and part-fill with potting soil. Place the pots of jasmine in the bucket, then adjust the level of the soil until the tops of the pots are just below the rim of the bucket. Take the plants out of their pots, and place them in the bucket. Fill in with potting soil and water well.

4 Push the willow shoots into the potting soil around the bucket edge, following the angle of the sides of the bucket. This will splay out the shoots so that when they are tied together at the top they will be gracefully bowed. Loosely tie the jasmine shoots to the willow with string, so that the string will not cut into the stems of the young plants. Tie the willow stems together, with string, about 12 inches from their tips. Other climbers, such as clematis and honeysuckle, could also be used for this project.

FAR RIGHT: *By cutting the willow stems when they are dormant and keeping the planting in a frost-free place, such as a sheltered doorway or conservatory, the willow shoots will root and become a living support for the jasmine.*

PROJECT: CONTAINER CONE

A LITTLE TIME AND EFFORT invested in making and planting this bulb cone in the fall will pay dividends in spring, producing an exuberant mound of color that will last for many weeks.

INGREDIENTS AND TOOLS
10-inch diameter terracotta pot
2 x 3 feet of 1 inch galvanized
   wire mesh
Wire cutters
Sphagnum moss
Soil-based potting soil
PLANTS
Muscari "Blue Spire" x 100

1 Using the wire cutters, cut out a semi-circle, radius 18 inches, from the mesh.

2 Form the wire into a cone shape, and tie the sides together by twisting the cut ends of the wire around themselves. Place the cone upside-down in the pot to hold it steady. Start lining the cone with

moss to a thickness of ¾–1¼ inches. Fill with approximately 2 inches of potting soil. Arrange a circle of bulbs, almost touching, on the soil, each with its nose pushing down and outward.

3 Work steadily up the cone in this way, adding moss, filling with soil, and placing a layer of bulbs every 1½ inches. Space the bulbs not more than 1½ inches apart. Cover the filled cone with moss, and secure it with a "lid" of wire mesh.

4 Fill the pot with potting soil and invert the completed cone onto it. The top inch or so of the cone is prone to drying out, so be sure to check regularly and water when necessary.

Pale pink scillas (above) and Muscari "Blue Spire" (right) are ideal subjects for this treatment, but do not be hesitant about experimenting with other small bulbs—dwarf narcissus or wood anemone, in particular, would look very striking.

PROJECT: *QUIRKY CONTAINERS*

1 Assemble the plants and materials, ensuring the cistern has drainage holes. Add a layer of gravel, followed by the potting soil. Plant the helictotrichon in the center, surrounded by the oxalis, plectranthus, and begonias. Water well.

2 Saw the wire into lengths long enough to circle the copper tubing twice, plus approximately 3 inches.

3 Bend a length of wire with pliers to form a short hook. Wrap the wire around the tubing twice, then pull the end of the wire through the hook, bending it

A TRIP TO A LOCAL JUNKYARD produced two unusual objects for containers—an old copper cistern and copper tubing.

INGREDIENTS AND TOOLS
Copper cistern and tubing
Gravel
Soil-based potting soil
Copper wire
Mini hacksaw and pliers
Plastic plant pot
PLANTS
Helictotrichon sempervirens x 1
Oxalis vulcanicola x 2
Plectranthus species x 2
Begonia rex cultivars x 3
Graptopetalum paraguayense x 2
Ceropegia woodii x 1

back on itself. Repeat at intervals down the tube. Push a plastic plant pot halfway down the tubing to act as a bung. Add potting soil to within 3–4 inches of the top of the tube. Plant the remaining plants, and firm in with potting soil.

RIGHT: ***A modern, architectural garden is the perfect home for this striking display.***

Project: *Bath Time*

In this witty scheme, a leaky antique bathtub is given a new lease on life as a surprisingly productive vegetable garden. Other large containers, such as enamel wash tubs or old-fashioned sinks, are also suitable.

Ingredients
Old tub
Soil-based potting soil
Small terracotta pots x 20
Willow shoots x 4

Plants
Lettuce varieties, such as "Red Salad Bowl," "Mantilia French," and "Royal Oakleaf," x 4 of each
Parsley x 2
Runner beans x 3

1 As the bath will be very heavy when filled with potting soil and plants, place it in its final position before you add the soil. Make sure there are sufficient drainage holes in the bottom.

2 Fill the bath with potting soil to within 1½ inches of the rim. Arrange the pots upside-down in a pattern in order to mark off the different planting sections.

3 Plant each lettuce variety in its own section and plant the parsley at the back.

4 Push in the willow shoots behind the parsley. Hoop one shoot across the others and tie to the upright shoots. Plant the beans at the base of the shoots.

LEFT AND ABOVE: *In time, the runner beans will cover the willow stems completely to transform the arrangement into an elegant garden sculpture, which would look as effective on a balcony as it would in a small yard. Pinching out the shoots regularly will keep the beans under control.*

PROJECT: *CORNER COLOR*

CORNER CONTAINERS add interest to awkward areas around the house.

INGREDIENTS

Corner container, 3 feet in height
Soil-based potting soil
Slow-release fertilizer

PLANTS

Orange-flowered *Abutilon* x *hybridum* x 1
Canna indica x 2
Mimulus aurantiacus x 2
Cuphea caeciliae x 2
Bidens ferulifolia x 3

1 Arrange the well-watered pots on the ground before planting. This makes it easier to see how you want to group them in the container. Obviously, large containers need large amounts of potting soil, and a false bottom helps to reduce the amount needed. A further saving can be made by rejuvenating last year's potting soil. Empty the soil into a wheelbarrow and add the required amount of slow-release fertilizer, following the manufacturer's instructions. Mix together thoroughly before returning to the container. Place the plants, still in their own pots, in the container, and adjust the level of the potting soil until the top of the deepest pot is just below the rim of the container.

2 Remove the plants from their pots by supporting the stem and rootball with one hand and tapping the pot rim on a firm surface.

3 Place the abutilon and canna, which form the main structure of the planting, in the center and at the back of the container. Place the mimulus, which will give an early focus of color, at center front, and the cuphea and bidens along the front; they will bush out and soften the edge of the container. Fill in with potting soil to within 2 inches of the rim of the container, and water well.

RIGHT: *The corner pot, with its rich and exotic scheme, is a dazzling focal point in a hitherto neglected part of the garden.*

The luxuriant and cascading splendor of a well-planted hanging basket will enhance any garden. Hanging baskets offer the gardener great scope for inventiveness and imagination. As well as manufactured wire baskets, there are many unusual objects, such as coconut shells, buckets, colanders, and vegetable baskets, that can be adapted to make effective containers. Although traditionally used to decorate doorways and porches, hanging baskets can play a more intimate role in the garden, suspended from an arbor or garden shed, or from the boughs of trees. Being imaginative with your choice and use of plants will result in more interesting displays, making hanging baskets objects of beauty in their own right.

Hanging Baskets

ABOVE: *A romantic, "castles-in-the-air" effect can be created with a two-tier basket. This color-themed arrangement uses both tender and hardy plants.*
LEFT: *A beautiful and abundant planting of* **Begonia** *x* **tuberhybrida** *"Diana Wynyard,"* **Helichrysum petiolare,** *and* **Plectranthus coleoides** *"Variegatus."*

TYPES OF HANGING BASKET

Conventional hanging baskets vary from 12–20 inches in diameter. The bigger the basket, the more voluptuous the effect, and plants will grow more vigorously and stay healthy longer in the extra potting soil. Flat-bottomed baskets are more stable for planting up, but they hold less soil.

You can replace the basket chains with colored cord to tie in with the colors of the flowers or foliage, or with the paintwork of the house or garden furniture. Make sure the cord is strong enough to support the weight of the full basket, however, and will not rot if continually wet.

There is considerable scope for improvisation. A terracotta pot can be turned into a handsome hanging container by drilling three holes beneath the rim and using cord or rope to hang it. Yard sales and junk shops can also yield unusual "baskets," from painted ceramic pots to birdcages.

USING HANGING BASKETS

Baskets are usually hung by doorways, singly or in pairs, to soften the harsh lines of the architecture, and make an entrance more welcoming. They can be used to set off features such as arbors or pergolas, or to decorate less attractive garden

structures such as sheds. Quirky, improvised baskets, however, are more appropriate for enclosed, intimate spaces, where their eccentricity will not look out of place. For an unusual effect, hang baskets among the lower branches of trees where they will dangle like large, exotic fruits. Vary the heights of the baskets, and use light-colored plants—*Tolmiea menziesii* "Taff's Gold," *Helichrysum petiolare* "Limelight," tradescantias, chlorophytums, white petunias, or impatiens—which will appear to glow in the shade.

Although hanging baskets are ideal for trailing plants, you can use almost any plant to great effect—from argyranthemums and abutilons, through hostas and heucheras to zauschnerias. For a rich, flamboyant planting, mix colors in a basket; for elegance and sophistication, keep to a single-color theme. Use plants with a graceful habit, dramatic leaf shape, or distinctive flowers that look good from below—the double-flowered, pendulous *Begonia* x *hybrida* "Pendula" combines all these qualities.

FOLIAGE SCHEMES

Foliage plays a crucial role in hanging basket displays, showing off flowers to maximum effect and giving substance to a planting. Large-leaved plants, such as *Hedera colchica* or *Pelargonium* "Chocolate Peppermint," will add weight and stature to arrangements. Use grasses like *Molinia caerulea* "Variegata" and *Felicia petiolata* to arch out over them.

To create a lighter look, you can use trailers with cut leaves or paler foliage: *Pelargonium* "Atomic Snowflake," for instance, or *Helichrysum petiolare*, *Anthemis punctata cupaniana*, *Senecio*

ABOVE: *Simple displays require simple backdrops. Bare woodwork gives these pelargoniums and their curved wire basket a chance to stand out.*
FAR LEFT: *Curled wire hooked onto zinc buckets adds a quirky touch to this improvised display.*

leucostachys, or *Bidens ferulifolia*. *Rhodochiton atrosanguineus* will twine its way up the chains of the basket to show off its dusky flowers, while *Tropaeolum peregrinum* used in the same way will produce a brighter and more cheerful effect.

WINTER INTEREST

Although flower color is in short supply during the winter, there is no reason to neglect your baskets. There are plenty of attractive evergreen plants that are able to withstand cold weather. Use ivy with varieties of *Vinca major* or *V. minor*

to trail gracefully and provide movement. Contrast the silvery *Cerastium tomentosum* with the dark green fingers of *Helleborous foetidus* and the leathery leaves of *Bergenia purpurea* to create a rich texture.

On their own, winter-flowering pansies can look bedraggled, but mixing them with evergreen foliage or the colorful shoots of cornus or willow will lift the display. A jumble of different-colored pansies can look harsh in the bleak winter garden, so use pure, single colors, if possible.

Other good choices for winter are: *Euonymus* "Silver Queen," with variegated foliage; *Euphorbia myrsinites*, with trailing stems of glaucous foliage; *Festuca glauca*, an upright blue grass; *Ophiopogon planiscapus* "Nigrescens," a black, grass-like plant, and *Iberis sempervirens*, with small evergreen leaves and white, scented flowers in spring.

PREPARATION AND MAINTENANCE

A well-planted hanging basket should be entirely smothered by flowers and foliage within a few weeks—and should stay that way. So it is well worth taking the time and making the effort to prepare and look after a basket properly.

BASKET LINERS

A good basket liner should allow air and water to penetrate, to keep the roots of the plants healthy. It should be easy to cut, enabling you to make planting holes where you choose. If you are using a liner with pre-cut holes, the holes should be able to accommodate plants of different sizes.

Hardy pansies, ivy, and lamiums will give a colorful display over a long season.

Sphagnum moss is the material traditionally used to line hanging baskets. However, although it meets all the practical requirements and looks attractive, increasing concerns about the exploitation of peat moss reserves have seen it supplanted in recent years by more environmentally friendly materials. One such example is coco-fiber. Neat and durable, coco-fiber can be shaped to fit any size of basket. To plant through it, all you need to do is cut holes with a pair of scissors. Coco-fiber linings will last only a year and should be discarded after this time (they will readily degrade on the compost heap). The third option is plastic liners. They do not biodegrade, but in their favor they are inexpensive and easy to cut to the required size.

ABOVE: *A bizarre-looking mix of echeverias and Agave americana "Variegata" proves that there are no limits to what you can grow in a basket.*
ABOVE LEFT: *With their healthy and vigorous growth, these petunias and brachycomes will soon disguise the basket liner.*

POTTING SOIL

Soil-based potting soils (see pages 15–16) are the best choice for hanging baskets since they give up their water reserve slowly. However, a large basket containing soil-based potting soil will be extremely heavy, so use equal amounts of soilless and soil-based potting soils to make a lighter mixture. Water-retentive gels (see page 17) will help maintain a good water supply.

FIXING THE BASKET

All hanging baskets must be securely fixed. For wall-hung baskets, drill and plug the wall, then screw in strong brackets. Holding an empty basket against the wall first will help you to gauge the correct position; the basket should be high enough to allow you to pass by without getting a faceful of wet foliage. The plants may grow approximately 9 inches out from the basket, so take this into account, too.

If the basket is to hang from a pergola or beam, either hook it to a rope tied around the wood, or screw a heavy hook into the wood and hang the basket from there.

To prevent a wall-hung basket from blowing around in the wind, push two thin canes horizontally into the body of the basket at the back. By forming a triangle with the wall as they rest against it, the canes act as an efficient brace.

PLANTING UP

Remove the chains, if possible, and sit the basket in a large flowerpot, or hang it at a workable height; though awkward, this method enables you to see how the display is developing as you plant.

Put a layer of sphagnum moss in the bottom and lay a piece of plastic sheet across it, dishing it slightly so that it will retain some moisture. For plastic liners, which are fairly moisture retentive, you can omit the sheet. If you are using coco-fiber, overlap the pieces so that no gaps are left, and trim any surplus from around the top before adding the sheet. You can either cut planting holes at this stage, before adding the potting soil, or make them one at a time as you plant your way up the basket.

Add the potting soil and start planting near the bottom of the basket with some plants that will spread widthways, others that will trail and give depth. Lobelias are good, reliable plants for in-filling. If you are using bedding plants, buy them in single rather than mixed colors, so that you will have more control over the color scheme.

Plant at regular intervals as you work your way around and up the basket, and use a good mix of plant types. Start to introduce larger plants from halfway up. Do not plant right to the top of the sides as water tends to run out of the plant holes near the rim without penetrating the soil; growth from the top will soon hide the baldness.

At the top, start around the edge, angling plants to encourage their foliage to cover the rim. Work inward, creating variety and contrasts by mixing foliage and trailing plants. Large baskets can sustain some larger plants, but will need plenty of water; make a depression in the soil's surface as you finish planting to help the water soak in.

WATERING

Do not water the basket until it has been hung, but thereafter remember to water frequently and regularly. To avoid having to climb onto chairs or up ladders with a watering can, either attach a hose to a broom handle, or use a lightweight, hand-held pump that pumps water up a hooked pipe and into the basket. There are compact pulley systems on the market that raise and lower the basket for you to water and deadhead.

With careful combinations of textures, colors, and forms, a richly planted basket becomes a garden in its own right.

PROJECT: *BACK TO NATURE*

MADE ENTIRELY from natural products, this hanging basket has a very rustic character. Once past its prime, it can be consigned to the compost heap where every part of it will eventually break down to return its goodness to the soil.

INGREDIENTS

10-inch diameter wicker basket
Sphagnum moss or woolen fleece liner
Soil-based potting soil
Stout clematis stems x 2
String

PLANTS

White petunias x 3
Nemesia fruticans x 3
Silene uniflora "Flore Pleno" x 3
Polygonum capitatum x 3

1 Assemble the plants and materials. Make sure the plants are well watered.

2 Line the basket with a thin, even layer of moss or fleece.

3 Fill the basket two-thirds full of potting soil, firming it down onto the liner.

4 Position the petunias and nemesia in the middle of the basket, with the silene and polygonum trailing over the sides. Carefully feed soil around the plants, firming in gently. Water well. Bend one end of a clematis stem around a handle and tie with string. Tie the other end to the opposite handle. Repeat with the second stem of clematis and the two remaining handles.

RIGHT: *Hanging from the branch of a tree, the basket is in perfect harmony with its surroundings, highlighted against a backdrop of green foliage.*

PROJECT: GREAT BALLS OF IVY

1 Remove the chains from one basket, and stand the other on a pot.

2 Line the chained basket with moss to approximately a third of the way up. Fill with potting soil, and firm to reduce settling. Using the wires as a guide, insert one ivy plant per section. Add moss and soil to two-thirds of the way up the basket. Insert a further two plants per section. Arrange them so that any long shoots will lie across the bare gaps. Finish lining with moss, and top up with potting soil.

3 Place the empty basket upside-down on top of the full one, then tie them together securely with wire.

4 Line the empty basket with moss through the wires, fill with potting soil, and plant ivies to correspond with those in the other basket. Squeeze the plastic pot in at the top, as a watering funnel. Hang the basket in position and water.

THESE BALLS OF IVY make adaptable garden decorations, either stylish and formal, or witty and irreverent, depending on how and where you hang them.

INGREDIENTS

18-inch diameter wire hanging
   baskets x 2
Sphagnum moss
Soil-based potting soil
Plastic-coated wire
2¾-inch diameter plastic pot
PLANTS
Ivy plants (*Hedera helix* "Minty") x 36

FAR RIGHT: *Ivy balls lend year-round elegance to garden recesses, entrances, and gateways. A fairly hard shearing-over every spring will keep them fresh and tidy.*

PROJECT: *FEAST OF FOLIAGE*

FOLIAGE OF DIFFERENT textures and tones with just a few flowers as highlights makes a stunning display.

INGREDIENTS AND TOOLS
18-inch diameter wire basket
Large plastic pot
Large plastic bag
Scissors
Sphagnum moss
Soilless potting soil

PLANTS
Pelargonium "Atomic Snowflake" x 1
Pelargonium "Decora Rose" x 2
Helichrysum petiolare x 2
Petunia "Pink Chiffon" x 4
Plectranthus coleoides "Variegatus" x 2
Silver-leaved *Begonia rex* x 1
Large-leaved begonia x 1
Purple-leaved *Begonia rex* x 1

1 Remove the chains from the basket, and stand it on the pot for stability. Cut a circle 10 inches in diameter from the bag.

2 Line the bottom third of the basket with a ¾–1¼-inch thick layer of moss. Place the circle on the moss, and cover with potting soil to just below the level of the moss. Press down firmly. Gently squeeze the rootballs of the trailing pelargoniums and helichrysum, then ease them through the wires or feed the foliage through from inside the basket.

3 Work up the basket, alternately lining with moss and filling with potting soil. Insert the remaining plants at irregular intervals, using the begonia leaves as a central focus. Stand back regularly to check the balance of the planting.

RIGHT: *In sun or dappled shade, this rich, leafy planting adds sophistication to an informal setting.*

GOOD WINDOWBOX PLANTING can transform a house, an apartment block, even an entire street. Even though an apartment's windowsill may seem very small to someone with grand gardening ideas, a well-planned windowbox can dramatically brighten an otherwise uninspiring outlook, while simple decorative techniques can transform a plain windowbox into an attractive focal point. Windowboxes also bring a welcome touch of greenery to urban areas where it is in short supply. In fact, for apartment-dwellers, a windowbox may well be the only place to grow vegetables and herbs. However, it is very important for a windowbox to be in sympathy with the style, material, and architecture of the house.

Windowboxes

ABOVE: *Try to match the character of a planting to that of the window. These pelargoniums are a charming complement to the bright red paintwork.*
LEFT: *A powerful display of vibrant pelargoniums against the dense, lush foliage of Virginia creeper.*

TYPES OF WINDOWBOX

Windowboxes are available in a range of materials—natural and man-made—and a variety of sizes to fit most sills. Buy the largest box your sill can take, as an undersized box can look lost. A narrow sill, or no sill at all, does not mean you cannot have a box; support it on brackets, instead.

As with baskets and pots, you can improvise windowboxes from household items. Empty food cans make cheap alternatives to manufactured boxes; wire them together for extra stability, and give them a coat of paint or varnish inside and out if you want them to last more than a year.

TERRACOTTA AND STONE

Terracotta is one of the most popular materials used for windowboxes—it looks good in any location, can be decorated in a number of ways, and suits both formal or informal plantings. The weight of a terracotta box makes it very stable but if there is a danger of it being dislodged, drill small holes at the back or sides and attach it with wires or nylon to hooks or vine eyes in the wall.

If the box is to be a year-round feature, make sure that the terracotta is frostproof. Terracotta also dries out rapidly, so you will need to water frequently—more so in hot or windy weather.

Stone and concrete troughs are too heavy to be used on sills, but can be placed on the ground or raised on improvised plinths of weathered brick, stone, or wood under ground-floor windows. Stark and bright when new, they weather with age to more attractive, mellow tones.

PLASTIC

Plastic windowboxes are inexpensive and easy to move around. Although relatively unobtrusive, they are not usually very attractive, but you can hide the dark brown and green versions easily enough by using trailing plants. Avoid white plastic, however, since this will show through even the most luxuriant of plantings. Used inside larger wooden or terracotta windowboxes, plastic boxes make excellent water-retentive liners.

WOOD

Wooden windowboxes are easy to make, which is a boon if you cannot find a ready-made one to fit the sill. Inserting a rigid plastic liner will help

Terracotta replicas of lead windowboxes are durable and relatively lightweight. This planting is deliberately kept simple so as not to detract from the decorative detailing on the box.

plain box, but will give a planting more interest as trailers begin to creep through them. Alternatively, nail thin dowel or rope onto the wood in a variety of patterns, or staple attractive mahonia or holly leaves or lengths of colorful willow or dogwood stems to the box. These will give a bright, rustic look that is particularly effective with winter plantings.

METAL

Galvanized boxes and wrought-iron and wire baskets make good, sturdy, and durable windowboxes. Untreated metal will need to be painted to prevent rusting, or given a coat of varnish. Galvanized tin, however, is already rust-proof and can be left untreated. It may look glaringly bright at first, but its shiny surface will gradually oxidize to an attractive, soft gray.

ABOVE: *A galvanized windowbox with a simple spring display of hyacinths and variegated ivy.* RIGHT: *A plain stone trough is the perfect foil for this lush planting of begonias, pelargoniums, trailing ivy, and plectranthus.*

keep the interior of the box dry, thereby extending its life. In addition, wooden windowboxes look appealing in almost any setting, whether traditional or modern, and can be made to look rustic or sophisticated with different surface treatments, such as varnish, stain, or paint.

Wooden boxes can be decorated in various ways. Use an electric jigsaw to cut a decorative edge or a series of ornamental holes in the sides. Making holes not only improves the look of a

USING WINDOWBOXES

Despite their name, windowboxes can be used in almost any setting—as freestanding troughs on a patio, for instance, or as decorative details, alternated with flowerpots, to outline a roof terrace. They also make good wall or shelf planters; fixed securely in staggered rows above one another, they can add colorful interest to a bare expanse of wall in a courtyard.

PLANTING SCHEMES

A successful windowbox planting has to fulfill a number of criteria: it needs to be in harmony with its immediate surroundings, and to have a structure that is strong enough to remain in good shape for several months. Cascades of color in the form of trailing fuchsias, ivy-leaved pelargoniums, and pendulous begonias will transform the exterior of a house, but the display must look good from inside as well. Bear in mind that plants in windowboxes tend to lean away from the

ABOVE: *This windowbox displays a sensitive use of color, despite containing many different plants, including diascias, bacopas, and petunias.*
ABOVE LEFT: *An abundance of herbs is as visually appealing as it is useful.*

window toward the light. Furthermore, for most of the day, incoming sunlight means the plants will be visible only in silhouette. By using plants with a strong architectural quality, such as cordylines, you can create bold shapes that will look striking whatever the time of day.

A windowbox can be planted specifically to complement a trough positioned below a ground-floor window. The two plantings do not have to be identical; they will look attractive if they echo each other while retaining their distinct characters. Using vertical forms such as *Anisodontea capensis* below and trailing forms such as *Convolvulus sabatius* above will encourage the plantings to grow into one another.

If you have no garden, a sunny windowsill is the ideal place to grow a few herbs. A small boxful is as decorative as it is practical; the widely varied leaf shapes and textures of parsley, marjoram, thyme, chives, oregano, nasturtiums, basil, and sage create attractive foliage combinations, and their sweet aromas will fill the air.

Fragrant plants are particularly important in windowbox plantings. The unmistakable scent of hyacinths and wallflowers in the spring, and allysums, *Verbena* "Loveliness," and stocks in the summer will be even more intoxicating carried in directly from a windowbox rather than diluted in an open garden.

As a windowbox planting is a decorative feature of your property, it should always complement its architecture. A formal townhouse with tall windows lends itself to a smart, formal planting, while a less restrained planting using a wider variety of shapes and textures would be more suitable for an informal location, such as a rustic, converted barn with windows of different sizes and shapes.

Although often hard to place, purple petunias combine well with helichrysum, verbenas, and lobelia. Each complements the other, as well as the house, to produce a stunning effect.

A cheerful windowbox display of white and yellow daffodils with trailing ivies provides welcome color in early spring.

The more formal the situation, the greater the need for symmetry in a windowbox planting. A dramatic, ordered arrangement of strong shapes makes a real impact against a large, imposing window, whereas a more informal planting of delicately colored flowers would simply be overshadowed.

An informal planting can be structured so that it appears to defy the space restrictions of the windowbox. By combining plants that arch and spread with upright and trailing varieties, you can build up a multi-layered mass of flowers and foliage tumbling and billowing out of the box.

SEASONAL PLANTING

Permanent, year-round structure can be provided by evergreens such as box, euonymus, hebes, and ivies. The effect can be changed each season by introducing bulbs, perennials, and annuals in succession. It is best to sink seasonal plants into the box in their individual pots, as moving plants in and out can disturb the permanent inhabitants.

Plants in a winter windowbox are exposed to severe conditions. If sheltered by an overhanging ledge, they are likely to get very dry; prolonged frosts create difficult growing conditions, while strong winds can be damaging since they buffet the plants with considerable force.

Tough evergreen plants with different leaf shapes and varying textures will make an interesting winter display that lasts: *Polypodium vulgare, Epimedium pinnatum, Iris foetidissima, Bergenia* "Abendglut," *Euphorbia myrsinites,* and *Hebe albicans* "Red Edge" are all ideal candidates. Underplanting with snowdrops and winter aconites will give you some color early in the year, while smaller varieties of daffodils—*Narcissus triandus, N.* "W.P. Milner," and *N. poeticus,* for example—will prolong the interest until the summer planting is due.

Mixed annuals like nemesias, candytuft, larkspur, and lobelias have a simplicity and charm, while free-flowering plants like bidens and felicia produce an airy effect. All of these plants would make ideal choices for a colorful and vivacious informal windowbox in summer.

PREPARATION AND MAINTENANCE

Whether you have a single windowbox or a number that form part of a grander planting scheme, good preparation is always worthwhile. With a little care you can grow strong, healthy plants that will form long-lasting displays requiring relatively little maintenance.

POTTING SOIL AND DRAINAGE

Windowboxes dry out rapidly, so use a soil-based potting soil, which retains water well (see page 15). Its weight will also help keep boxes stable.

Good drainage is essential. Make sure there are plenty of holes in the bottom of the box, and check occasionally to ensure they have not been blocked by packed soil or roots; clear them from below with a stick, if necessary. If the box is raised, place 2 inches of gravel in the bottom to act as a sump until the excess water drains away.

Check boxes regularly. It is easy to assume that a windowbox gets watered every time it rains, when, in fact, no water may reach it at all, if it is sheltered by an overhang, for example, or if the wind blows the rain in the opposite direction.

An upstairs windowbox should be placed on a tray so that you can water it without splashing passers-by below. Raising the box on small blocks will prevent it becoming waterlogged.

Raising this water trough off the ground and drilling drainage holes provides a free-draining container for **Anthemis punctata cupaniana.**

POSITIONING AND FIXING

A windowsill may be the most obvious place to site a windowbox, but it may not be the most practical if the sill slopes, or if the windows open outward. Securing the box on brackets is a good solution. When you come to position the brackets, remember that you will need to be able to reach the box easily to water, weed, deadhead, and prune. Also, it is better to plant the box *in situ* through an open window, rather than struggling up a ladder laden with a planted box.

It is essential to use strong, well-secured fittings to support the windowbox. Bolting or screwing the box to these is another safety measure worth taking. Attach brackets to the wall using wall plugs and brass or zinc screws that will not corrode, but get advice from a professional builder before you drill into rendered walls.

PROJECT: *ON THE EDGE*

Press the silver leaf (still attached to its backing) onto the size, and rub firmly on the backing with your fingertips or soft brush until the leaf sticks evenly to the size. Peel off the backing paper. Repeat for the entire rim, patching any gaps with left-over scraps of leaf.

3 Leave to dry completely overnight. Smooth over the leaf with a soft brush to remove any loose pieces, and press the leaf more tightly to the base. Fill the windowbox to a third of the way up with potting soil. Add the plants, filling around them with potting soil and firming in well. Water thoroughly.

A COAT OF SILVER can lift a commercially produced container out of the ordinary and, as here, inspire a distinctive planting scheme. Jars of size and silver, gold, and bronze leaf are available from artists' supplies stores.

INGREDIENTS
Terracotta windowbox, 18 x 7 x 7 inches
Jar of size
Sheets of silver leaf
Soft paintbrush
Soil-based potting soil
PLANTS
Artemisia stelleriana x 3
Viola "Molly Sanderson" x 1
Salvia officinalis "Purpurea" x 2

1 Assemble the plants and materials.

2 Apply a coat of size with a brush to the rim of the windowbox, which must be clean and dry. Leave for 30 minutes.

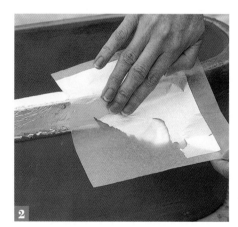

RIGHT: *A sophisticated purple and black planting scheme, with silver highlights, deserves to be prominently displayed, perhaps on a windowsill at the front of the house or on a large garden table.*

PROJECT: *SHELF LIFE*

THIS SHELF gives you the flexibility to change plants as often as you like, to create new schemes, or simply replace those plants that are past their best.

INGREDIENTS AND TOOLS
6-inch diameter clay pots x 5
Cardboard
Treated wood, measuring 10 x 36 x 1 inch
Brackets x 2
External wood paint
Paintbrush
Pencil
Electric drill and jigsaw
1½-inch screws and plugs
Spirit level
Soilless potting soil
PLANTS
Pelargonium "Eclipse Red" x 5

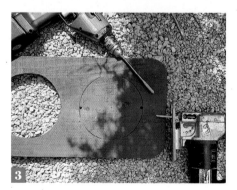

1 Assemble the plants and materials. Cut out a cardboard circle slightly smaller than the outside diameter of the top of the pot. Paint the brackets and the wood.

2 Draw a central line along the length and width of the piece of wood. Using these two lines to guide you, center the cardboard template and draw a circle. Mark out four more evenly spaced circles.

3 Drill through the board, just touching the inside of one circle. Insert the jigsaw blade into the hole and saw around the circle. Repeat for the four other circles. Screw the brackets onto the shelf at convenient points, and hold the shelf in position on the wall; use a spirit level to ensure it is horizontal. Mark the position of the screw holes on the wall, and remove the shelf. With a masonry bit, drill the holes in the wall. Tap in the plugs, replace the shelf, and screw it to the wall. Add potting soil to the pots, and plant the pelargoniums. Place the pots in the holes.

RIGHT: *This simple shelf is an attractive alternative to a windowbox where there is no windowsill, and it allows you to see the wonderful patina that has built up on the clay pots.*

PROJECT: *WOODLAND PLANTER*

STAPLING TWIGS ONTO a wooden box or planter creates a colorful and rustic container for a woodland-style planting.

INGREDIENTS AND TOOLS

Treated wooden box, measuring
 42 x 8 x 8 inches
Willow stems (*Salix daphnoides,*
 S. alba "Vitellina," and "Britzensis")
Hand pruners
½-inch galvanized staples
Hammer
Coarse gravel
Soilless potting soil

PLANTS

Iris foetidissima x 1
Asplenium scolopendrium cristatum x 2
Polypodium vulgare x 2
Helleborus foetidus x 2
Galanthus nivalis x 20

1 Cut the stems into 8-inch lengths. Mark two parallel lines along the box, about 1½ inches in from either edge. Using the lines as guides, fix stems of an even thickness to the box with the hammer and staples. Stagger the staples to ensure closer coverage. Staple longer, pliable stems across the front of the box to form patterns.

2 Spread a layer of gravel in the box for drainage. Fill with potting soil.

3 Place the iris in the center of the box, with the ferns and hellebores symmetrically to either side, and intersperse with snowdrops. Firm in with more potting soil and water well.

RIGHT: *This evergreen planting will be effective throughout the year, with seasonal highlights of white snowdrops and scarlet iris seed pods.*

N<small>OT ONLY MUST</small> plants grown in containers be good solo performers, providing several layers of interest by way of flower, form, and foliage, they also need to work well in combination with other plants. Some of the entries in this directory are old favorites, but I have also given unconventional subjects and suggestions for unusual combinations, proving that the scope for creative container planting is limited only by your imagination.

KEY TO SYMBOLS

✳	Hardy	☁	Shade
ⅎ	Half-hardy	🌢	Hanging basket
⌂	Tender	🗠	Windowbox
❀	Sun	▽	Small pot
☁	Partial shade	🧺	Large pot

Plant Directory

A<small>BOVE:</small> *A soothing Mediterranean scheme of succulents and blue-gray **Omphalodes luciliae** is given an injection of color by the miniature red rose.*
L<small>EFT:</small> *These rustic baskets provide the strong structure necessary to prevent their abundant plantings from looking wild and undefined.*

Numbers in brackets indicate plant hardiness zones. Plants that are not given numbers are best considered annuals.

SHRUBS AND CLIMBERS

ABUTILON

Producing maple-like leaves and showy, pendant, bell-shaped flowers, abutilons are strong-growing, reaching 6½–10ft in height. Plants can be kept smaller by cutting back hard annually, or by taking cuttings in summer to produce new plants. With their robust upright growth, they are good for forming the framework of a planting; the large leaves add strength to architectural arrangements, and give structure to frothier plantings. "Silver Belle" (9–10) has white flowers, "Canary Bird" (9–10) soft yellow, and "Nabob" (9–10) deep red. *A. pictum* "Thompsonii" (9–10) has delicate-looking, yellow mottled leaves and orange flowers.

ARTEMISIA "POWIS CASTLE" (5–8)

This small evergreen shrub, 3ft high, with finely cut, silver-gray foliage, gives a hot, dry effect and looks especially good with yellows and purples, and against broad or strap-like leaves. Use it with purple sage (*Salvia officinalis* "Purpurascens" [4–9]) and *Penstemon* "Alice Hindley" (7–9). Tolerant of drastic pruning, it can be kept small.

CUPHEA (CIGAR FLOWER)

Grown mainly for their attractive flowers, cuphea species bring subtle touches of orange to planting schemes. *C. ignea*

The delicate orange flowers of Cuphea caeciliae *add warmth to an arrangement of argyranthemums and mimulus.*

(9–10) is a fresh green plant that produces orange-red tubular blooms, each with a white rim, non-stop throughout the summer. The variegated form has yellow mottled leaves, which show up well in dappled light. Both forms will grow to 2ft in height. *C. caeciliae* (9–10) is a vigorous and bushy plant with orange and red flowers on red stems, and is a good provider of dark green foliage for backing orange or red schemes.

FUCHSIA

Fuchsia flowers range from the sublime to the ridiculous, from overblown, many-petaled monsters to the most exquisite soft orange, green-tipped tubular blooms. "Red Spider" (9–10) is a graceful, half-hardy hanging basket plant, trailing 18–24in, whose uncomplicated red flowers with long narrow sepals and shorter petals produce a rich effect. In complete contrast, the tender "Thalia" is an upright grower, 2–3ft high, and a star in its own right, with dramatic, dark red-green, downy foliage. Its flowers are long, narrow red tubes held in clusters at the end of the shoots. *F. magellanica* "Versicolor" (8–9) has leaves of pink, gray, white, and green that create a symphony of color with the fine pendulous drops of its deep red flowers, and its effect cannot be overstated. It is ideal for large containers, reaching a height of 2½ft and a spread of 3ft. "Marinka" (9–10) is a half-hardy trailing variety with dark green leaves and dark red flowers that makes a solid base planting for a hanging basket. "Golden Marinka" (9–10) is its variegated form. Low-growing, to 4in, and half-hardy, *F. procumbens* (9–10) is very unfuchsia-like, with unusual upright flowers of yellow, brown, green, and blue, and large, shiny fruits. Tender *F. fulgens* (9–10) has soft orange, tubular flowers with green-tipped sepals and large, pale green leaves. The young foliage has a frosted appearance. It can grow up to 6ft tall, though it will rarely reach this height when confined to a container, and is well suited to large displays and exotic backyard-jungle effects.

LAVATERA MARITIMA (9–10)

Like a more subtle version of an hibiscus, *L. maritima* has large, lilac trumpet flowers with a dark center and soft, sage-green foliage. It will grow to 5ft, but can be kept within bounds by cutting back hard. Use it with pinks like *Osteospermum* "Pink Whirls" (9–10), or contrast it with bold foliage and dark flowers, such as *Cosmos atrosanguineus* (6–9) and *Sedum telephium maximum* "Atropurpureum" (3–9).

LOTUS HIRSUTUS (5–8)

A delightful shrub, 10–24in high, with softly hairy, small silver-gray leaves. The tight heads of its pea-like flowers are white with a subtle pink tinge, and are followed in fall by conspicuous, shiny red-brown seed pods. Try it with other "woolies" such as *Stachys byzantina* "Silver Carpet" (4–7), or *Lagurus ovatus*, the furry hare's-tail grass.

PLEIOBLASTUS VIRIDISTRIATUS (5–9)

Although many bamboos are extremely tall, vigorous plants, they can be grown successfully in containers if given good conditions. They enjoy a rich potting soil that is kept moist but not necessarily wet. Less vigorous than many, *P. viridistriatus* can be cut back each spring and, if fed well, makes a thicket of 3ft-high shoots. Its green and yellow striped leaves brighten shady areas, though it is equally happy in full sun.

SOLANUM

Related to the potato, these plants make vigorous growers for large containers. *S. jasminoides* (7–10) is potentially a very large climber, 16ft and taller, but young plants from cuttings are more likely to make 6–8ft. It produces clusters of small, pale blue flowers, which are particularly effective when allowed to scramble through a planting and out of the pot. "Album" is the delightful white form. *S. laciniatum* (9–10) deserves a large pot on its own. It is a robust plant, 4–5ft high, with very deeply cut leaves and blue flowers, followed by orange seed pods that hang like small eggs. It is easily grown from seed or cuttings. Vigorous and cheerful, *S. rantonnetii* (10) is a bright green bush, growing to 5ft high, bearing blue flowers with a yellow eye. Try combining it with *Osteospermum ecklonis* "Blue Streak" (9–10) or the large-leaved hedychiums.

PERENNIALS AND ANNUALS

AGAPANTHUS

These classic container plants, growing up to 3ft high, are guaranteed to make an impressive sight with their broad, strap-like leaves and great umbels of flowers. There are many named varieties, giving a range of flower colors from the rich deep blue of *A.* "Storm Cloud" (8–10) through the mid-blue of *A.* "Headbourne Hybrids" (7–10) to *A.* "Bressingham White" (7–10). The darkest varieties of blue look stunning contrasted with clear yellow flowers such as *Argyranthemum* "Jamaica Primrose" (9–10) or *Coreopsis verticillata* "Moonbeam" (3–9).

ANTHEMIS PUNCTATA CUPANIANA (5–9)

A vigorous, mat-forming perennial, 12in high, with white, yellow-eyed daisies that grow on short stems over finely cut, silvery foliage. Its vigor may overwhelm lesser plants, but despite this it has an elegant appearance, and can be cut back hard if necessary. Use it to trail over the side of a pot or from a hanging basket, where, combined with pink argyranthemums or tangled with *Convolvulus althaeoides* (6–8), it will create a light, romantic effect. For a contrast, grow it with *Tradescantia zebrina* (9–10).

ARGYRANTHEMUM (MARGUERITE)

The epitome of a summer container plant. Clouds of flowers are produced right through the season on this bushy, evergreen woody perennial with fresh green, deeply cut leaves. Argyranthemums are easy to propagate, fast growing (reaching 3ft), and will soon fill a large container. They also make impressive standards. Shear off the fading heads to encourage new flower buds. "Jamaica Primrose" (9–10) is a vigorous plant with wonderful large, clear yellow daisy flowers. "Vancouver" (9–10) has double pink flowers that develop a large central boss, while *A. gracile* "Chelsea Girl" (9–10) has white daisy flowers over fine, thread-like, gray-green leaves. On their own they create a misty, romantic effect, but give still greater impact if used with bold foliage. Try a mixed planting with *Osteospermum* "Whirlygig" (9–10), *Phormium tenax* "Purpureum" (8–10), and *Verbena bonariensis* (7–10).

ARUM ITALICUM "Pictum" (6–9)
Rich green, spear-shaped leaves, boldly
marbled with gray or pale green, make this
one of the most exciting herbaceous plants
for winter effect. The leaves appear in fall,
reaching a height and spread of 12in, and
die away in spring. Plants will need shelter
from strong winds. Combine with *Bergenia
purpurascens* (5–8) or the holly-like leaves
of *Osmanthus heterophyllus* (7–9).

✽ ☀ ☁ 🪴 🗄 ⊽ 🧺

BEGONIA
This is a genus that embraces extravagantly
flowered plants, such as the tuberous
varieties of begonia with their enormous
double flowers, as well as some of the most
subtle and delectable of foliage plants. In
crowded, still conditions a few begonias
can be susceptible to mildew, but this is
easily controlled with an occasional spray
of fungicide. *B. semperflorens* has flowers
in red, white, and pink, and leaves in green
or shiny bronze. The plants are compact,
12in high, with fleshy stems and leaves,
and are ideal for interplanting in hanging
baskets and windowboxes to give an early
mature look. *B. rex* hybrids have large,
characteristically begonia-shaped leaves
patterned with pink and purple, many
with silver speckling. They range in height
from 8–16in. *B. sutherlandii* has dainty
clusters of soft orange flowers, which look
good with the foliage of *Helichrysum
petiolare* "Limelight" (9–10). It dies back
in winter, and can be propagated from
tubers produced on the stems. Grown in
pots, it will make a trailing mound up to
1–2ft high and wide. The *B.* x *tuberhybrida*

*Begonias in soft pastel colors are ideal for
lightening shady areas of the garden.*

Pendula Group are robust plants, 1½–2ft
tall, which hang well from baskets. Choose
the slightly double varieties in yellow or
white, and hang in baskets where they will
be back-lit by the morning or evening sun
to make the planting glow. *B. fuchsioides* is
an upright plant, 2–4ft high, with small,
serrated, glossy leaves and small, red
flowers produced almost continuously.
Its strong, reddish-colored stems give a
good vertical line, so use it as the central
plant in a group and contrast it with larger,
softer leaves.

BIDENS FERULIFOLIA (8–10)
A feathery plant that reaches a height and
spread of 2–3ft, *B. ferulifolia* produces
warm yellow flowers on thin stems. Its
wind tolerance makes it a useful trailer for
hanging baskets, where it will scramble
among other plants, putting up its bright
flowers here and there. It is easily rooted
from cuttings. Use it with yellow or red
cannas and croscosmias.

CONVOLVULUS
Relatives of the invasive bindweed,
convolvulus make colorful, sun-loving
scramblers when confined to a pot. The
hardy *C. althaeoides* (6–8) has finely cut
leaves of silvery green, long trailing stems,
and large, pink trumpet flowers that open
in the sun. It grows to 2–3ft, and can be
planted to trail or to climb up a support;
stand pots on a hard surface to prevent the
vigorous roots establishing themselves in
the ground and putting up new shoots.
Low-growing and non-invasive, *C. sabatius*
(8–9) has cheerful, blue-purple flowers

throughout the summer, and small, fresh green leaves on trailing stems 6–8in long. It is tolerant of a degree or two of frost.

COREOPSIS VERTICILLATA

"MOONBEAM" (3–9)

Delicate, primrose-yellow daisy flowers are combined with dark, hair-like foliage on a distinctive plant, 1½–2ft tall, that looks equally good growing alone or combined with the grassy leaves of *Molinia caerulea* "Variegata" (4–8).

COSMOS ATROSANGUINEUS (6–9)

This is a very striking plant that produces maroon flowers on long stalks late in the season, and grows to a height of 18in. For winter protection, the tuberous root can be lifted and stored in a frost-free place, as you would a dahlia. The flowers have the scent of cocoa, and are sometimes so dark they appear as intriguing little black holes, an effect that can add interest to a pedestrian planting. Good as a partner for *Argyranthemum gracile* "Chelsea Girl" (9–10).

CROCOSMIA

Not an obvious choice for containers, but, given the shortage of orange-, red-, and yellow-flowered plants with distinctive foliage, crocosmias can be very useful. The flower spikes appear late in the summer, but the upright, sword-shaped leaves make a good impression throughout the season. The variety "Lucifer" (5–9) is 3ft tall, with intense red flowers. "Citronella" (5–9) has golden-yellow flowers, and "Solfaterre"

(5–9) pale apricot-yellow, with attractive, dusky bronze foliage. Both grow to 1½–2½ft in height. Grow with cannas or hedychiums to create a jungle-like effect.

DAHLIA

The continued hybridizing of dahlias has led to an almost infinite range of sizes and colors. The dwarf varieties, at 12in high, are easier to manage in a pot than the large border types, but lack their stature and presence. Grow the tall varieties in large pots for a dashing and colorful display on a grand scale. They need plenty of water, so are best grown without competition from other plants. Place them out of strong winds, and overwinter the tubers in a frost-free place. "Bishop of Llandaff" (7–9), with its exceptional purple foliage and intense red flowers, grows to 3ft high. Plant it with white cosmos, *Argyranthemum gracile* "Chelsea Girl" (9–10) or, for an intense red arrangement, with *Canna* "America" (7–10).

DIASCIA

A greater number of diascia hybrids are now becoming available. All are free-flowering, and elegant shades of pink. *D. vigilis* (7–9) is a pretty, gentle plant with spikes of flowers on dainty, airy stems and leaves of soft, fresh green. *D. rigescens* (8–9) has distinctive, coppery-pink flowers and, with its tough, toothed leaves, is more rugged-looking. Both plants grow to a height of 12–18in. *D.* "Lilac Belle" (7–9) is a small-flowered, more compact variety, just 9in high.

EUCOMIS BICOLOR (9–10)

This is a solid-looking plant, consisting of a substantial rosette of broad, wavy-edged leaves from which rises a dense spike of pale green flowers topped, pineapple-like, by a rosette of bracts. Reaching an eventual height of 18in, it looks best when contrasted with lighter and wispier subjects.

FELICIA

These are evergreen perennials with daisy-like flowers. *F. amelloides* (9–10) carries, from late spring to fall, an abundance of yellow-eyed, sky-blue flowers on long stalks above the foliage. The small foliage itself makes little impact, so deadhead by shearing to encourage more flowers. Plants grow to a height of 12in. *F. a.* "Santa Anita" (9–10) has larger flowers on a more robust-looking plant. "Reads White" (9–10) is the white variety. *F. petiolata* (8–10) is a very different plant and much hardier, withstanding several degrees of frost. It has soft, gray-green leaves on stems that arch out, and small pink flowers. Mix it in with stronger foliage, and use it in hanging baskets and to trail its way out of boxes and pots.

FESTUCA GLAUCA (4–9)

A useful small, clump-forming grass, 4in high, with stiff, intense blue-gray leaves. Divide a clump and put small sections among other plants to "spike up" the textural quality of an arrangement. Try juxtaposing it with the purple, fleshy leaves of *Sedum* "Bertram Anderson" (5–9).

GAZANIA

These gay, sun-loving plants, 8in high, have large, daisy-like flowers in brilliant shades of red, orange, and yellow, which open in the sun. The foliage may be gray or green. Though perennials, they are usually grown as seed-raised annuals, but named varieties can be propagated from cuttings in late summer. "Cream Beauty" (9–10) is a more subdued color than most and has gray-green, downy leaves. It is useful on its own or with strong, clear blue flowers, such as those of *Convolvulus sabatius* (8–9).

HAKONECHLOA MACRA "Aureola" (5–9)

This bright green and yellow striped grass, making a dense clump of arching leaves 12in high, adds a light, graceful feel to a planting. It associates well with a range of colors, including white petunias, acid yellow *Coreopsis verticillata* "Moonbeam" (3–9), soft yellow *Argyranthemum* "Jamaica Primrose" (9–10), apricot *Mimulus aurantiacus* (8–10), and *Lobelia* "Lilac Cascade." Use it as a main plant with other, smaller plants to cover the rim of the planter.

HEDYCHIUM (ginger lily)

These are impressive foliage plants with exciting, showy flowers, good for bold foliage arrangements and for creating a jungle-like effect. *H. gardnerianum* (7–9), 5–6½ft tall, produces spikes of soft yellow and red flowers in late summer. *H. densiflorum* (7–9), a smaller variety at 3–5ft, has ribbed foliage and soft orange flowers in dense spikes.

HELICHRYSUM PETIOLARE (9–10)

This is one of the top ten plants for containers, providing a firm but graceful base to a planting. It has trailing stems, sweeping out horizontally, and small, heart-shaped, gray, felted leaves that look good in any color scheme. "Limelight" (9–10) is particularly effective with soft, clear oranges, for example, *Begonia sutherlandii* and the pale forms of *Mimulus aurantiacus* (8–10). The heads of the creamy yellow flowers on long stalks can be a distraction, so cut them off, if you prefer, and prune the whole plant occasionally to stop it swamping smaller displays.

HELICTOTRICHON SEMPERVIRENS (4–9)

This dense clump of blue-gray, upright leaves, 2–3ft high, makes a useful evergreen feature plant for a large container. Try it with pink *Argyranthemum foeniculaceum* (9–10), which complements its narrow foliage, or with the felted leaves of *Helichrysum petiolare* (9–10).

HOSTA

These handsome, clump-forming plants, producing flowers of lilac or white on upright stems, positively thrive when grown in pots. Leaves vary from 12in across in *H. sieboldiana* (3–9), to only 1–2in in *H. venusta* (3–9). Many forms have bold variegation, and some make a bright show of yellow as the leaves die back in the fall. *H.* var. *albopicta* (3–9) is 2ft high, with young leaves of bright yellow and green that color briefly in fall to orangey yellow. *H.* "Krossa Regal" (3–9)

is a large plant with a height of 1½ft and spread of 2½ft, blue-green leaves, and tall spikes of lilac flowers. *H. lancifolia* (3–9), with shiny, dark green, narrow, pointed leaves, gives a lighter, more grassy effect than the larger-leaved types. Perhaps the ultimate in large hostas, *H. sieboldiana* var. *elegans* (3–9) has rounded, blue-gray leaves, deeply veined and puckered, and short heads of very pale lilac flowers. Feed it well and it can reach a height of 3ft and spread of 5ft. *H. sieboldii* (3–9) has lance-shaped leaves with a narrow white edge, and grows to 18in. Hostas are ideally suited to light shade; use them in foliage combinations with ferns and bamboos to create a cool restful refuge in the garden. If you have to use slug pellets, place them under the leaves in the pot away from pets.

IMPATIENS (busy lizzie)

These bushy evergreen annuals with succulent stems and flat, spurred flowers are effective if used sparingly. The reds tend to be from the blue end of the spectrum, making them difficult to use with true reds and yellow-reds. The pure white varieties give a very cool, fresh feel, enhanced by the plant's moist, fleshy quality. Quite different is *I. niamniamensis*, an upright, fleshy-stemmed plant with red or yellow parrot-bill flowers. It makes an exciting addition to the backyard jungle.

INCARVILLEA

A genus that includes plants with very different characters, from the showy and exotic to the graceful and dainty. *I. delavayi* (5–8) is an easy plant, 2ft high,

Set against a backdrop of greenery, the intense bluey-red flowers of impatiens have an eyecatching brilliance.

useful for giving a lush effect. From its clump of deeply divided, crinkly leaves arise stout, erect stems holding aloft several robust, pink trumpet flowers. It benefits from some protection in winter. In contrast, *I. sinensis* "Cheron" (8–10) has fine, fern-like foliage and more delicate, creamy-white flowers on 2ft-long scrambling stems. Treat it as tender. Grow it with *Solenopsis axillaris* to produce a misty, transparent effect.

✳ ⌂ ☀ ♠ ▦ ⛶ ⛾

LAGURUS OVATUS (HARE'S-TAIL GRASS)

A curious little annual grass with soft "hare's tails" flowerheads at the top of fine, 18in stems. It is easily propagated from seed. Try it with *Begonia rex* cultivars or succulent crassulas.

✳ ☀ ♨ ▦ ⛶ ⛾

LOBELIA

The annual *L. erinus* is one of the cheeriest, most useful, and, if looked at closely, most beautifully flowered plants. Low and narrow-leaved with compact or trailing habit, it is covered in dainty flowers right through summer to fall. The bushy varieties reach a height and spread of 6in, trailing ones 9in. Plants range in color from red, pink, and blue to lilac and white, and are invaluable as fillers in all plantings, covering the potting soil until the larger plants spread out. The *L. erinus* "Cascade" series of trailers is useful in hanging baskets. They are suitable for mixing with almost any other plants, but lilac "Cascade" with *Verbena* "Loveliness" (7–9) or *Nemesia caerulea* (9–10) looks particularly striking. It is hard to believe the half-hardy perennial *L. tupa* (8–10) is related to the annual lobelia. It can reach 3–5ft, and the stems, sprouting light green, downy leaves, are topped with a spike of two-lipped, red-brown flowers. Somberly effective with *Stachys byzantina* "Silver Carpet" (4–7) and *Coreopsis verticillata* "Moonbeam," it is best suited to larger pots.

⌂ ⚔ ☀ ♠ ▦ ⛶ ⛾

LOTUS BERTHELOTII (8–10)

This evergreen has fine, silvery leaves and striking, scarlet flowers resembling upturned claws in summer. The soft, feathery stems will trail to 2–3ft, making this an excellent choice for hanging baskets. Use it with *Petasites albus* (4–8) for contrasting leaf texture and matching color.

⌂ ☀ ♠ ▦ ⛶ ⛾

MELIANTHUS MAJOR (8–10)

A magnificent gray-green foliage plant. The large leaves are deeply cut into numerous leaflets, each sharply toothed along the margin. Plants can reach 6½–10ft in height, but more often will attain only half that size in a container. They do not always flower when pot-grown but, given the foliage, that is of little consequence; they look stunning with the chocolate *Cosmos atrosanguineus* (6–9). When crushed, the leaves smell of a strange and not always pleasant mixture of rubber and peanut butter. Cut leggy growth back in spring.

⚔ ☀ ♨ ⛾

MIMULUS AURANTIACUS (8–10)

The soft colors of the flowers are the primary reason for growing this plant. Growth can be somewhat straggly, but it is usually self-supporting, reaching a height of 1½–2ft. The pale buff and pale apricot forms are ideal for adding lightness to a scheme. Soft orange *Begonia sutherlandii* and pale green *Helichrysum petiolare* "Limelight" (9–10) make good partners, as do any pure blues and yellows.

⚔ ☀ ⛶ ⛾

MOLINIA CAERULEA "Variegata" (4–8)
An elegant and most useful grass, growing to 18in high, with narrow, arching leaves striped creamy yellow. Spikes of tiny purple flowers wave from the top of cream stems in late summer. It adds softness to a planting; try it with the blue-flowered *Felicia amelloides* (9–10) or with *Trifolium repens* "Purpurascens Quadrifolium" (4–8).

NEMESIA
N. caerulea (9–10) is a very pretty, bushy little plant, easy-going and cheerful, growing to 8in and producing a cloud of small lilac flowers on an upright stem. It will flower up to the first hard frost, so shear off those flowers that are spent to encourage a new flush. *N. denticulata* "Confetti" (8–10) is similar but hardier, and its flowers have crimped petals that add to its charm. Delightful for creating a light feel and when planted with *Verbena* "Loveliness" (7–9) or *Oxalis vulcanicola* (9–10). A small pot full of the cheery little annual *N.* "KLM," with its sky-blue and white flowers, makes an eye-catching display. Plants reach a sprawling 9–12in.

OPHIOPOGON PLANISCAPUS
"Nigrescens" (6–9)
This black-leaved plant is a gem and an absolute boon to the container gardener. Its diminutive size, just 8in, belies the impact it can have. Leathery, shiny, narrow leaves sprout from easily divided tuberous roots. Black shiny berries in late summer are a bonus. Good with succulents, gray foliage, and just about any flower color.

ORIGANUM LAEVIGATUM (5–8)
A sun-loving, herbaceous perennial that reaches 18in in height. It has a distinctively delicate appearance: from a compact clump of small, gray leaves shoot wiry, red stems, branching into a misty spray of purple-pink flowers from midsummer onward. It associates particularly well with gray foliage, and makes an excellent partner for the furry gray leaves and pale yellow flowers of *Stachys byzantina* "Silver Carpet" (4–7) or the smaller-leaved *Lotus hirsutus* (5–8).

The natural affinity between red pelargoniums and clay pots guarantees stunning results.

OSTEOSPERMUM
These plants produce large, daisy-like flowers that open in response to the sun. An ever-increasing number of varieties provide a range of colors that includes white, pink, blue, yellow, and purple. Many have petals that are differently colored on the reverse. Some have an upright habit, others are more spreading, but all make excellent container plants, giving a cheerful, summery effect. Cuttings are easily rooted during late summer. *O. ecklonis* "Blue Streak" (9–10) is an upright plant, 18in high. Its white flowers have blue centers and are blue on the reverse. Also upright, *O.* "Buttermilk" (9–10), 2ft high, has dark-eyed, soft yellow flowers. Both varieties create a fresh, cooling effect. *O. jucundum* (9–10) is a low-growing spreading plant, 12in, which will spill out of a container. It produces soft mauve flowers in good numbers during summer and autumn.

PELARGONIUM
Pelargoniums offer a very wide range of flower colors and leaf shapes, so much so that you could create startlingly varied displays using pelargoniums alone. Varieties whose flowers are less showy than those of traditional "geraniums" more than make up for it with attractive, scented foliage. "Mabel Gray," 1½–2ft tall, has lemon-scented, deeply cut, stiff, rough leaves that give a very busy effect. "Chocolate Mint," the most wonderful plant, reaches a height of 1½–2ft and a spread of 2–3ft. Its large, shallow-lobed, rounded, velvety leaves measure 6in across and have a dark splash in the middle, and

are spread around and out of the pot by thick, hairy stems. The foliage has a strong scent of peppermint when crushed. *P.* "L'Elégante" is a variegated, ivy-leaved, trailing pelargonium, growing to 2ft, with white-edged leaves that give the plant a succulent appearance. The pale mauve flowers are subdued enough to be a good complement to the busy foliage. Both *P. crispum* and *P.c.* "Variegatum" are stiff, upright plants, 1½–2ft tall, whose charm comes from the small, aromatic, crinkly foliage. *P.* "Atomic Snowflake"—an awful name for a wonderful plant—grows 12in high. Its mounds of pale, rounded leaves, gently variegated and scalloped, sit softly and comfortably at the edge of a planting.

PENSTEMON

Upright, shrubby plants, 1½–2ft tall, with narrow, lance-shaped leaves. Their trumpet-shaped flowers, ranging from cherry red to dark purple, provide a wealth of color from midsummer until late fall. When pot-grown, penstemons are best treated as half-hardy. Plants are easily propagated from late summer cuttings. "Eureka White" (7–9) has white trumpet flowers, "Midnight" (7–9) very dark violet-purple. "Alice Hindley" (7–9)—a dream of a plant—has large, dusty lavender and white flowers that combine beautifully with silvery foliage. "Stapleford Gem" ("Sour Grapes") (7–9) is a curious mix of blue and gray-purple.

PETASITES

Excellent foliage plants, with large, bold leaves. Far too invasive to let loose in the garden, but tamed in a pot, *P. japonicus*

"Variegatus" (3–8) is an exciting and majestic plant. When well nourished, the round leaves, splashed and streaked with an irregular yellow variegation, can reach 2ft or more across. Try planting it with a large grass such as *Helictotrichon sempervirens* (4–9) or the bamboo *Pleioblastus viridistriatus* (5–9). It can also be used to stunning effect in very large hanging baskets. *P. palmatus* (3–8) is a vigorous grower, although it reaches a height of only 12–18in, with jagged-fingered leaves that give it a unique character. Use on its own or as a foil for lighter, more airy plants. The leaves of *P. albus* (4–8) are silver, almost white, when young, while older leaves are green above, intense silver below. At 12in in height, it is a less vigorous species than those mentioned above, but is a useful plant where plain but effective foliage is needed.

PETUNIA

Though breeders have improved petunias' resistance to bad weather, these annuals will perform better if provided with some shelter from the wind, reaching heights of 12–18in. Many of the colors available are harsh and difficult to use, in particular the striped varieties. However, two useful single colors are soft pink "Chiffon Morn" and pure white, of which there are several varieties. Buying single colors rather than mixed will give you more control over the planting scheme. Try one of the white varieties of petunia with *Tolmiea menziesii* "Taff's Gold" (7–9) and *Hakonechloa macra* "Aureola" (5–9), or use "Chiffon Morn" with *Pelargonium* "Atomic Snowflake."

PHORMIUM (NEW ZEALAND FLAX)

These evergreens are extremely useful in providing a bold vertical line and giving structure to a planting. If, faced with planting a large container, you are wondering where to start, place a large phormium in the center to spark off ideas. *P. tenax* "Purpureum" (8–10) has stiff, upright, sword-shaped, purple-green leaves. It is potentially a tall plant, to 8ft, but will remain smaller in a container. *P.t.* "Bronze Baby" (8–10) is a smaller version, growing to 2ft, with wine-red leaves. *Melianthus major* (8–10), *Petasites japonicus* "Variegatus" (3–8), and *Argyranthemum frutescens* all make good companions.

RHODOCHITON ATROSANGUINEUS

This classy climber, with dark purple, hanging tubular flowers, will reach a height of 6½–10ft. Left unsupported, it will trail. Although a perennial, it can easily be raised from seed each year. It makes a novel plant for hanging baskets, and the foliage of *Artemisia* "Powis Castle" (5–8), *Helichrysum petiolare* (9–10), or *Plectranthus coleoides* "Variegatus" all help show off the flowers.

SALVIA

This vast family encompasses a wide variety of plants of diverse sizes and colors, many of which are useful to the container gardener. *S. coccinea* "Cherry Blossom" ("Coral Nymph") is a light and graceful salvia, 12in high, with open tiers of white and pink flowers. Treat it as an annual and grow with *Petunia* "Chiffon

Morn" or *Pelargonium* "Preston Park." *S. confertiflora* (9–10) is a large and distinctive plant, growing to a height of 4ft. Its green leaves with brown undersides and small, red-brown flowers packed on a tall, red, velvety flower spike make an impressive sight in late summer. Use it alongside strong foliage plants like zantedeschia, or go the opposite way and surround it with the frothy frizz of white *Argyrantheum foeniculaceum* (9–10). *S. patens* (8–9) has flowers of a very penetrating gentian blue. It grows to 18in high, and from early sown seed it can be flowering by midsummer. A simple planting using *S.p.* "White Trophy" (8–9) and the pale blue *S.p.* "Cambridge Blue" (8–9) makes a very effective display. *S. farinacea* (8–9) is an upright plant with spikes of small, violet-blue flowers on velvety stems, 1½–2½ft high. The variety "Strata" (8–9) has violet-blue flowers with a white calyx, producing an appealing two-tone effect, and foliage with a gray sheen. "Alba" (8–9) has mealy white flowers that associate well with *Helichrysum petoliare* (9–10) and *Senecio maritima* "Silver Dust" (8–10). *S. cacaliifolia* (8–10) is a vigorous plant, 1½–2ft high, ideal for trailing over the sides of pots. It has royal blue, narrow, tubular flowers and deltoid, finely hairy leaves. Use it in combination with other intense colors or with white agapanthus. *S. elegans* (8–10) is a sprawling plant, growing to a height of 1½–2ft, with charming, bright red, tubular flowers and leaves that smell of pineapple when crushed. Easily rooted from cuttings taken during the summer, it is most useful for large containers, where its vigor can be accommodated against the bold, broad

leaves of zantedeschias or *Pelargonium* "Chocolate Mint."

SCAEVOLA AEMULA "BLUE WONDER"
A trailing annual, growing 1–1½ft long, and covered in small, fan-shaped, rich blue flowers. It is a durable plant that will flower until the frosts, and is ideal for growing in hanging baskets, where the flowering stems can be seen at their best.

SENECIO
A genus of plants whose leaves range from white felt to blue-gray succulent, through the green "beads" of *S. rowleyanus*. *S. viravira* (9–10) is a vigorous, spreading plant with silvery white, much divided leaves, growing to a height of 1½ft and a spread of 3ft or more. The flowers are insignificant creamy tufts. It is happy to trail over the edge of pots or scramble its way up through stronger plants, and may need pruning to prevent it over-running lesser plants. It makes a good foil for strong colors such as *Dahlia* "Bishop of Llandaff" (7–9) and *Phormium tenax* "Purpureum" (8–10). *S. maritima* "Silver Dust" (8–10) is more compact and feathery, with a height and spread of 12in. Pinch out the weed-like flowerheads. For a filigree effect, grow it with *Verbena bonariensis* (7–10) and *Origanum laevigatum* (5–8).

SOLEIROLIA SOLEIROLII
(MIND-YOUR-OWN-BUSINESS) (9–10)
A vigorous, spreading carpet of tiny leaves, 2in high, making a neat "ground cover" among other plants in pots but just as

attractive grown on its own. It can be easily tamed with a pair of scissors. Although evergreen, it can be turned brown by frost. The variety "Argentea" has variegated leaves that give the plant a gray appearance. "Aurea" has fresh yellow-green foliage.

SOLENOPSIS AXILLARIS
This dainty plant, reaching 8–12in in height, has fine leaves and narrow-petaled, pale blue, star-shaped flowers. It has a slightly scrambling habit, but set among bolder plants it will have a softening effect. It provides plentiful amounts of seed. A related white variety is available.

SPHAERALCEA MUNROANA (4–7)
Soft hairy leaves provide the perfect setting for small, pink, mallow-like flowers that are produced all summer long. *S. munroana* will spread and hang delightfully from a hanging basket or windowbox, reaching 18in. Make the most of its gentle, summery feel by growing it with similar charmers, such as *Tulbaghia violacea* (7–9) or blue *Convolvulus sabatius* (8–9).

STACHYS BYZANTINA
"SILVER CARPET" (4–7)
Use the silvery-gray woolly leaves of this non-flowering stachys in small arrangements as a foil for brighter colors and as a contrast to glossy foliage. It grows 6–7in high and dislikes winter wet.

Vigorous growth and abundant bright flowers make Tropaeolum majus *one of the most cheerful container plants.*

TOLMIEA MENZIESII "TAFF'S GOLD" (PICK-A-BACK PLANT) (7–9)

A supremely decorative plant, growing up to 18in in height, with mottled variegation on ivy-shaped leaves and intriguing tiny green and brown flowers in spring, which should be snipped off as they go over. Ideal in dappled shade, where it almost glows, and good with yellows and for adding light to an arrangement. Pendulous yellow begonias, white or blue lobelias, and *Trifolium repens* "Purpureum Quadrifolium" all make excellent companions. It is easily propagated from the young plants that form at the base of the leaf.

TRADESCANTIA

These evergreen trailing plants with oval, pointed leaves are useful for hanging baskets or when allowed to scramble around among more substantial plants. They grow to 6in high, will trail almost indefinitely, and are easily propagated from cuttings. *T. zebrina* (9–10) has dark leaves with glistening stripes that lighten the overall effect. *T. fluminensis* "Variegata" (9–10) is similar in form, but its leaves are light green and variegated, giving a spring freshness to an arrangement.

TROPAEOLUM

A genus of brightly colored plants that includes the familiar nasturtium. All tropaeolums make equally good trailers or climbers, and the abundance of flowers in warm colors manage never to look gaudy or garish. One rule, however: do not use them with reds at the blue end of the spectrum. *T. peregrinum* is a dainty, yellow-flowered climber with pretty, lobed leaves. It grows to a height of 5–6½ft. *T. tuberosum* (7–9) is a climber of considerable distinction with gray-green, gently lobed leaves. It will climb 6½–10ft and the flowers, a blend of yellow, orange, and red, with a long spur, are held aloft on long stems, giving an exotic look. Overwinter the tubers in a frost-free place. There are several varieties of the vigorous and showy *T. majus* (nasturtium), both compact and trailing. Colors range from pale yellow "Peach Melba" to the sultry dark crimson flowers and dark foliage of "Empress of India." "Alaska" is a bushy variety, with leaves irregularly splashed cream. Expect the bushy varieties to grow to 8–12in, the trailing varieties 3–6½ft.

TULBAGHIA VIOLACEA (7–9)

A summer-flowering delight with narrow foliage and delicate, dainty heads of pink flowers on 18in stems. The grassy foliage looks particularly good with black *Ophiopogon planiscapus* "Nigrescens" (6–9). This plant will tolerate a degree or two of frost.

VERBENA

These colorful plants—many of which are deliciously scented—have a long flowering season. Deadhead regularly to encourage new flower buds. "Silver Anne" (7–9) is a spreading perennial with small, serrated leaves and large, rounded heads of small, pink, fragrant flowers all summer.

"Loveliness" (7–9) has good heads of lilac flowers and a lovely scent. It will flower until the frosts. Both varieties grow to a height and spread of 18in or more. *V. bonariensis* (7–10) is very different. Its narrow, sparse, rigidly upright stems, growing to 5ft high, are topped with tufts of purple-blue flowers from midsummer through fall. It is very useful for growing through more lax plants, or for defining the vertical line of a planting. Take cuttings to perpetuate named varieties. Good summer companions are *Argyranthemum gracile* "Chelsea Girl" (9–10) and *Osteospermum* "Pink Whirls" (9–10).

ZANTEDESCHIA AETHEOPICA

(ARUM LILY) (8–10)

The arum lily has good architectural qualities of leaf and flower. Erect, arrow-shaped leaves on stout stems and white spathes are produced in early summer. After flowering, the leaves maintain their quality. Plants do not always need to be kept wet, and will tolerate a few degrees of frost. Use with other equally bold foliage to create a sumptuous planting with a tropical feel.

BULBS

ALLIUM

These onion relatives range in color from white and yellow through to blue and purple. One of the most striking varieties is *A. cristophii* (4–8), which has large, round heads of star-like purple flowers in summer, and grows 12–24in tall. It produces a marvelous effect coming up through *Helichrysum petiolare* "Limelight" (9–10).

CROCUS

Growing just 1–3in tall, these cheerful, early spring-flowering plants are ideal in permanent plantings to start the season, and, densely planted in small pots, provide bright splashes of color. After flowering, the grassy foliage is unobtrusive. Two distinctive varieties are *C. chrysanthus* "Cream Beauty" (4–9), a warm shade of cream, warmed still further by orange stigmas, and *C. c.* "Blue Pearl" (4–9), a cool lavender-blue with a yellow center.

GALANTHUS (SNOWDROP)

Snowdrops make charming highlights among dark foliage. Try them with the beet-red leaves of *Bergenia purpurascens* (4–8). Early spring-flowering plants, they grow from 4–12in. *G. elwesii* (4–8) is a chunky plant, with broad, strap-like glaucous leaves, while *G.* "Atkinsii" (4–8) is graceful, dainty and single-flowered.

GALTONIA (7–9)

This hardy bulb sends up tall stems, 3–4ft high and hung with substantial white bells, to make a stately plant for late summer effect. Plant it to come up through zantedeschia or melianthus. The variety *G. viridiflora* (7–9) is slightly smaller and has bells of a deliciously cool, pale green.

MUSCARI BOTRYOIDES

(GRAPE HYACINTH) (2–8)

Very common but reliable and attractive blue-flowered plants that flower in spring and grow to a height of about 4in. Mix them with evergreens or plant them in a pot of their own. "Album" (2–8) is the white form—very hardy and extremely classy.

NARCISSUS (DAFFODIL)

Tough and ideal for container growing, daffodils will cheer up the dreariest corner of the garden. Heights range from 3–18in and colors from rich egg-yolk yellow to glistening white. Try mixing pale varieties with clipped box or yew for a sophisticated effect. "Thalia" (4–9), 15in high, has delicate, pale yellow flowers best seen against a dark evergreen background. "Tête à Tête" (6–9) is a dainty plant, 9in high, with small, richly colored flowers two or three to a stem. It is ideal for a spring-flowering windowbox.

TULIPA (TULIP)

Tulips come in a bewildering range of shapes and sizes, but all are suitable for container-growing. Parrot tulips, 1½–2ft tall, have large flowers and fringed and flared petals, and make a particularly flamboyant display. *T.* "White Triumphator" is a white, lily-flowered tulip, growing to 2ft, with reflexed petals and considerable style. It flowers in late spring. *T. batalinii* "Bright Gem" (3–8) is a small, early spring-flowering tulip with soft yellow petals washed with orange, set among blue-tinted leaves. It will reach a height of 4–12in.

SUCCULENTS

AEONIUM ARBOREUM
"Arnold Schwarzkopff" (10–11)
Shiny black rosettes of succulent leaves
make this branching perennial a striking
plant, either on its own or as part of a
"dry garden" arrangement. It will grow
up to 3ft tall.

AGAVE AMERICANA
(century plant) (9–11)
Although agaves eventually become
enormous plants, young plants can be
contained in pots for many years at more
manageable heights of 6–30in. Their large
rosettes of tough, fleshy leaves each finish

*The characterful flowers of echeverias will
complement any planting scheme.*

with a very sharp spine—notice the pattern
of spines that each leaf presses into the
other. There are two variegated forms,
one striped yellow, the other gray.

CEROPEGIA WOODII (10–11)
An easily grown and intriguing trailing
plant, hanging to 2–3ft, with heart-shaped,
silver-green mottled leaves on wiry stems
and unusual, un-showy pink flowers. Older
plants develop dense swags of stems. It is
an unusual plant for adding a vertical line
to a planting, and unique in its coloring.

ECHEVERIA
Echeverias have distinctive rosettes of
fleshy leaves that rest on the ground, some
softly hairy (*E. pulvinata* [9–11]), others
with wavy or crinkled leaf margins

(*E.* "Aquarius" [9–11]), and ranging in
color from flesh pink to purple-blue.
Exotic pink and yellow flowers are
produced along erect stems, ranging in
height from 2–18in. Mix them with other
dry-looking plants such as *Lotus hirsutus*
(5–8), *Lotus maculatus*, *Festuca glauca*
(4–9), and *Ceropegia woodii* (10–11), or
try them with lush foliage plants such as
Nemesia caerulea (9–10), *Fuchsia
procumbens* (9–10), and cultivars of
Begonia rex.

SEDUM
Hardy and possessing considerable
character, sedums are good plants for
the front of a planting. The variety
S. maximum "Atropurpureum" (3–9) has
smooth, fleshy leaves of dark maroon and
flat heads of densely packed, small red
flowers that lend the plant a somber,
heavy feel. It combines well with cheerier
and lighter plants, such as pink
Sphaeralcea munroana (4–7), and will
reach a height of 18in or so. *S.* "Bertram
Anderson" (5–9) is a small plant, 4in high,
with wonderful deep purple foliage and
ruby-red flowers.

SENECIO KLEINIA (10–11)
A vigorous, spreading succulent with
leaves resembling juicy blue pencils
covered in a gray bloom. It is tolerant of
being grown in a wide range of conditions
and with a diverse selection of plants. Use
with hairy-leaved plants that contrast with
its smoothness, or let it scramble with
Tradescantia zebrina (9–10).

INDEX

Page numbers in italics indicate illustrations. Numbers in brackets denote hardiness zones. Plants not given numbers are best considered annuals.

Abutilon 23, *25*, 39, 55, 82
   A. x *hybridum* 50, *51* (8–10)
Acaena "Glauca" 35 (5–8)
Aeonium arboreum "Arnold Schwarzkopff" 93 (10–11)
Agapanthus 23, *24*, 83
Agave americana (century plant) 93 (9–11)
   "Variegata" *57* (8–10)
Ajuga reptans "Atropurpurea" 35 (3–8)
Allium 92
   A. christophii 38 (4–9)
allysums 71
Anisodontea capensis 70 (9–10)
annuals 14, 72, 83–92
Anthemis
   A. punctata cupaniana 32, 55, 73, 83 (5–9)
Aralia elata 28 (4–9)
architectural plants 22–3
Argyranthemum (marguerite) 55, 83
Artemisia
   A. "Powis Castle" *41*, 82 (5–8)
   A. stelleriana 74, 75 (3–8)
Arum italicum "Pictum" 84 (6–9)
arum lily (*Zantedeschia aetheopica*) 92 (8–10)
Asplenium scolopendrium cristatum 78, 79 (4–8)
automatic watering devices 18

bacopas 36, *70*
bamboo 23, *28*
bark 15
basket liners 56–7
baskets *80*

bathtubs 48, *49*
bay 26, 28
Begonia 69, 70, 84, *84*
   B. x *hybrida* "Pendula" 55
   B. rex 24, 46, *47*, 64, *65*, 84
   B. sutherlandii 25, 84
   B. x *tuberhybrida* "Diana Wynward" 52, 84
Bergenia
   B. "Abendglut" 72 (4–8)
   B. purpurea 56 (5–8)
Bidens 72
   B. ferulifolia 32, 50, *51*, 55, 84 (8–10)
bonemeal 16
borders 29
bougainvillea *19*
box *12*, 26, *27*, 32, 38, 72
brachycomes 57
buckets 42, *43*
bulbous pots 32–3
bulbs 14, 18, 39, 92
busy Lizzie (*Impatiens*) 55, 86, *87*

camellias 16
candytuft 72
Canna 29
   C. indica 50, *51* (7–10)
capillary action watering *17*
century plant (*Agave americana*) *57*, 93 (9–11)
Cerastium tomentosum 56 (3–8)
Ceropegia woodii 38, 46, *47*, 93 (10–11)
chlorophytums 55
cigar flower (*Cuphea*) 82
clematis 39
climbers 82–3
climbing plants 39
coco-fiber 57
cocoa shells 15
color *20*, 24–5
concrete troughs 68
Convolvulus 84–5
   C. sabatius 70, 84–5 (8–9)
cordylines 70
Coreopsis verticillata "Moonbeam" 24, 85 (3–9)

corner containers 50, *51*
Cornus 56
   C. stolonifera "Flaviramea" 39 (2–8)
Coronilla glauca 38 (8–9)
Correa backhouseana 24 (9–10)
Cosmos atrosanguineus 85 (6–9)
Crocosmia 85
Crocus 92
Cuphea (cigar flower) 82
   C. caeciliae 50, *51*, 82, *82* (9–10)

daffodils (*Narcissus*) 39, *45*, 72, *72*, 92
Dahlia 28, 85
deadheading 19
design 21–9
detergent 16
Diascia 36, 70, 85
   D. vigilis 32 (7–9)
drainage 18, 73
drought-tolerant plants 14
dry plantings 38
dryopteris 38

Echeveria 24, 28, 57, 93, *93*
Epimedium pinnatum 72 (4–9)
Eucomis bicolor 85 (9–10)
Euonymus 35, 72
   "Silver Queen" 56 (5–9)
Euphorbia 13
   E. cyparissias 41 (4–9)
   E. myrsinites 56, 72 (5–9)
evergreens 13, 34, 38, 72

feeding 16
Felicia 73, 85
   F. amelloides "Read's White" 36, 85 (9–10)
   F. petiolata 36, 55, 85 (8–10)
ferns 13, 38
fertilizers 15, 16
Festuca glauca 56, 85 (4–9)
   "Silver Sea" 40, *41* (4–9)
fixing hanging baskets 58
fixing windowboxes 73
flat containers 32
flowerpots 32

foliage 22, 23–4, *23*, 36, 40, *41*, 55, 64, *65*
foliar feed 16
formal plantings 26–8, 72
fragrance 71
frost 11, 18, 28
Fuchsia 39, 70, 82

Galanthus (snowdrop) 39, 72, 92
   G. nivalis 78, *79* (3–8)
Galtonia 92 (7–9)
galvanized windowboxes 69, *69*
garden soil 16
Gazania 13, 86
ginger lily (*Hedychium*) 23, 26, 28, 86
Glechoma hederacea 36 (5–9)
grape hyacinth (*Muscari botryoides*) 92 (2–8)
Graptopetalum paraguayense 46, *47* (9–10)
grasses 14, 55
Gunnera chilensis 28 (8–10)

Hakonechloa macra "Aureola" 86 (5–9)
hanging baskets 17, 52–65
hardy perennials 13–14, 26
hare's-tail grass (*Lagurus ovatus*) 34, 87
Hebe 24, 72
   H. albicans "Red Edge" 72 (7–10)
Hedera (ivy) 28, 56, 69, 72, *72*
   H. colchica 55 (6–9)
   H. helix "Minty" 62, *63* (6–9)
Hedychium (ginger lily) 23, 26, 28, 86
Helichrysum 71
   H. petiolare 32, 36, 39, 52, 55, 64, *65*, 86 (9–10)
   H. petiolare "Limelight" 55 (9–10)
Helictotrichon sempervirens 14, 46, *47*, 86 (4–9)
Helleborus foetidus 56, 78, *79* (4–8)
herbs 14, *70*, 71
heucheras 55

holly 26, 38
honeysuckle 39
hoof and horn 16
hornbeam hedge *28*
Hosta 14, 22, 23, 34, 55, 86
hyacinths 36, *69*, 71

Iberis sempervirens 56 (3–4)
Impatiens (busy Lizzie) 55, 86, *87*
Incarvillea 86–7
    I. delavayi 29, 86–7 (5–8)
informal plantings 72
Iris foetidissima 72, 78, *79* (7–8)
ivy (*Hedera*) *28*, 55, *56*, 62, *63*,
    69, 72, *72*

jasmine 39
Jasminum polyanthum 42, *43*
    (8–10)
Jerusalem sage (*Phlomis*
    fruticosa) 14, 38 (8–9)

Lagurus ovatus (hare's-tail grass)
    34, 87
lamiums *56*
larkspur 72
Lavatera maritima 36, 83 (9–10)
lemons *14*
lettuce 48, *49*
lilies *20*
lime 15, 17
liners 11, 56–7, 68–9
liquid feeding 16
Lobelia 34, 36, 71, 72, 87
    L. erinus 87
    L. tupa 87 (8–10)
Lotus
    L. berthelotii 38, 87 (8–10)
    L. hirsutus 36, 38, 83 (5–8)
Lysimachia nummularia 35
    (3–9)

maintenance 39, 56, 73
marguerite (*Argyranthemum*)
    55, 83
Mediterranean plants 14, 38
Melianthus 23
    M. major 87 (8–10)
metal containers 11, 24, 69

microclimates 26
Mimulus aurantiacus 50, *51*, 87
    (8–10)
mind-your-own-business
    (*Soleirolia soleirolii*) 90 (9–10)
Molinia caerulea "Variegata" 14,
    55, 88 (4–8)
monochromatic plantings 36
mulch 17
Muscari
    M. "Blue Spire" 44, *45* (4–8)
    M. botryoides (grape
       hyacinth) 92 (2–8)
myrtle (*Myrtus communis*) 14,
    26, 38 (8–9)

Narcissus (daffodil) 39, 45, 72,
    72, 92
    N. poeticus 72 (4–9)
    N. triandus 72 (3–8)
    N. "W.P. Milner" 72 (3–8)
nasturtiums 32
Nectaroscordum siculum
    bulgaricum 38 (4–9)
Nemesia 72, 88
    N. caerulea 88 (9–10)
    N. fruticans 23, 60, *61* (9–10)
New Zealand flax (*Phormium*)
    26, 89
nitrogen 16

olive oil cans *11*
Omphalodes luciliae 81 (4–9)
Ophiopogon planiscapus
    "Nigrescens" 36, 40, *41*, 56, 88
    (6–9)
Origanum laevigatum 88 (5–8)
Osmanthus 38
    O. delavayi 38 (7–9)
    O. heterophyllus 38 (7–9)
Osteospermum 13, 88
Oxalis vulcanicola 46, *47*
    (9–10)

pansies 27, 56, *56*
parsley 48, *49*
passion flower 26
Paulownia tomentosa 28 (6–9)
pedestal urns 32

Pelargonium 13, *28*, 55, 88–9, *88*
    "Atomic Snowflake" 55, 64,
       65, 89
    "Chocolate Mint" 55, 88
    "Decora Rose" 64, *65*
    "Eclipse Red" 76, *77*
    "The Crocodile" *41*
    windowboxes *66*, 67, *69*, 70
Penstemon 89
perennials 13–14, 26, 83–92
Petasites 89
Petunia 25, 89
    hanging baskets 55, 57, 60, *61*
    monochromatic plantings 36
    P. "Brass Band" *11*
    P. "Pink Chiffon" 64, *65*
    windowboxes *70*, 71
Phlomis fruticosa (Jerusalem
    sage) 14, 38 (8–9)
Phormium (New Zealand flax) 89
    P. tenax "Purpureum" 26, 89
       (8–10)
phosphate 16
Phygelius aequalis "Yellow
    Trumpet" *24* (7–9)
pick-a-back plant (*Tolmiea
    menziesii* "Taff's Gold") 55, 91
    (7–9)
plastic containers 11, 68
Plectranthus 32, 46, *47*, 69
    P. coleoides "Variegatus" 36,
       52, 64, *65* (9–10)
Pleioblastus viridistriatus 83
    (5–9)
Polygonum capitatum 60, *61*
    (4–8)
polymer gels 17
Polypodium vulgare 38, 72, 78,
    79 (5–8)
pots *30*, 31–51, *31*
potting 18–19
potting soil *8*, 15–16, 57, 73
pruning 38, 39
Prunus lusitanica 38 (7–9)

rainwater 17
repotting 18–19, *18*
Rhodochiton
    R. atrosanguineus 55, 89

rhododendrons 16
roof gardens 29
root-rot 18
rose *81*
rosemary 38
runner beans 48, *49*

Salix alba "Britzensis" 39 (2–8)
Salvia 20, *28*, 89–90
    S. argentea 21 (5–9)
    S. officinalis 74, *75* (5–9)
Scaevola aemula "Blue Wonder"
    90
Scarborough lily (*Vallota
    speciosa*) 29, 38 (8–10)
scillas 45
seasonal planting 72–3
sedges *13*
Sedum 93
sempervivums *24*, 34
Senecio 90
    S. kleinia 93 (10–11)
    S. leucostachys 55 (8–10)
    S. viravira 32, 90 (9–10)
shapes 22–3
shelves 76, *77*
shrubby germander (*Teucrium
    fruticans*) 38 (8–10)
shrubs 13, 82–3
Silene uniflora "Flore Pleno" 60,
    61 (3–8)
sinks 36
slow-release fertilizer 16
snow 28
snowdrop (*Galanthus*) 39, 72,
    78, *79*, 92
soil-based potting soils 15,
    16–17, 57, 73
soilless potting soils 15, 16
Solanum 83
Soleirolia soleirolii (mind-your-
    own-business) 90 (9–10)
Solenopsis axillaris 90
Sphaeralcea munroana 90 (4–7)
sphagnum moss 57
Stachys byzantina "Silver
    Carpet" 90 (4–7)
standards 26, 28, 39
stocks 71

stone containers 11, 68, *69*
succulents 14, 22, 38, *81*, 93
sunflowers *26*

terracotta 10–11, *10*, 24, 28
  flowerpots 32
  hanging baskets 54
  painting *9*
  windowboxes 68, *68*
Teucrium fruticans (shrubby
  germander) 38 (8–10)
Tolmiea menziesii "Taff's Gold"
  (pick-a-back plant) 55, 91 (7–9)
Tradescantia 32, 55, 91
trailing plants 36

Tropaeolum 91
  T. majus 91
  T. peregrinum 55, 91
troughs 11, 68
Tulbaghia violacea 91 (7–9)
Tulipa (tulips) 14, *15*, *33*, 38, 92
  T. batalinii 38 (3–8)

underplanting 14, 38, 72

Vallota speciosa (Scarborough
  lily) 29, 38 (8–10)
Verbena 71, 91–2
  V. bonariensis 37, 92 (7–10)
  V. "Loveliness" 71, 92 (7–9)

Versailles tubs 28, 32
Vinca
  V. major 55 (4–8)
  V. minor 55 (4–8)
vine prunings 39
Viola "Molly Sanderson" 74, 75
  (4–8)
Virginia creeper *66*

wall pots 33
wallflowers 39, 71
water-retentive gels 17, 57
watering 16–18, 19, 58
willow stems 39, 42, *43*, 48, *49*
windowboxes 66–79

winter
  care 19
  plantings 14, 38–9, 55–6, 72
winter-flowering pansies 56
wood
  containers 11, *32*
  planter 78, *79*
  windowboxes 68–9
wood anemone 45

yew 26, 38
yuccas 38

Zantedeschia aetheopica (arum
  lily) 92 (8–10)

ACKNOWLEDGMENTS

Author's acknowledgments
I would like to give my special thanks to Valerie Christie who typed the manuscript, and to Mr and Mrs R Paice for their permission to use their garden at Bourton House, Bourton-on-the-Hill, Moreton-in-Marsh, Gloucestershire, for photography. Thanks also to Keith Finlay of Rowborough Farm, Stretton-on-Fosse, Warwickshire for the wicker baskets photographed on pages 60-1, and to Kate Langley for letting us use her home to photograph the silvered windowbox planting project on pages 74-5.

Publisher's acknowledgments
The publisher would like to thank the following photographers and organizations for their kind permission to reproduce the photographs in this book:
2-3 Juliette Wade (Sparrowhall); 5 Camera Press; 6-7 Jerry Harpur (Bourton House); 9 J C Mayer - G Le Scanff (Chaumont-sur-Loire, Laurence Claude); 12 Vincent Motte (Lafourcade); 13 Gary Rogers; 14 Gary Rogers; 15 John Glover (Vann, Surrey); 19 Brigitte Thomas (Walda Pairon); 20 J C Mayer - G Le Scanff (La Closerie, Normandy); 21 Andrew Lawson (Gothic House); 22 Clive Nichols (Bourton House); 23 Marijke Heuff (Hadspen); 24 Andrew Lawson (Pots & Pithoi, Sussex); 25 The Garden Picture Library (Marijke Heuff); 26 left The Garden Picture Library (John Glover); 26-7 Michèle Lamontagne; 27 right The Garden Picture Library (Marijke Heuff); 28 left John Glover (Vann, Surrey); 28 right Juliette Wade (Will Giles); 29 Brigitte Thomas (Timothy Vaughan); 30 J C Mayer - G Le Scanff (La Closerie, Normandy); 31 The Garden Picture Library (Lorna Rose); 32 Jerry Harpur (Sonny Garcia, J Di Faustino); 33 Paul Williams (Bourton House); 34-5 Jerry Harpur (Anne Alexander-Sinclair); 34 left Clive Nichols (Bourton House); 35 right Andrew Lawson (Barter's Farm Nurseries); 36 Clive Nichols (The Old Rectory, Berks); 37 Clive Nichols (Bourton House); 38 Anne Hyde; 52 Marianne Majerus; 53 S & O Mathews (Upper House); 55 Brigitte Thomas (Jane Newdick); 56 Michèle Lamontagne; 57 right Michèle Lamontagne; 57 left J C Mayer - G Le Scanff (Les Forrières du Bosc); 58-9 S & O Mathews; 66 Michèle Lamontagne; 67 Charles Mann (C Butte); 68 John Glover; 69 below Andrew Lawson (Bourton House); 69 top J C Mayer - G Le Scanff; 70 left John Glover (Chelsea Flower Show 1992); 70 right Andrew Lawson; 71 John Glover; 72 John Glover; 73 Andrew Lawson (John Brookes); 80 Derek St Romaine (Chelsea Flower Show 1995); 81 Andrew Lawson (Bourton House); 82 Clive Nichols (Bourton House); 84 The Garden Picture Library (Marijke Heuff); 87 The Garden Picture Library (Marijke Heuff, Mien Ruys Garden); 88 John Glover; 91 The Garden Picture Library (J S Sira).

The photographs on the following pages were taken specially for Conran Octopus by Georgia Glynn-Smith: 1, 8, 10, 11, 16, 17, 18, 39, 40-51, 54, 60-5, 74-9.

The publisher would also like to thank Lisa Cussans and John Elsley.

Index compiled by Indexing Specialists, Hove, East Sussex BN3 2DJ.